T0361211

SIZE MATTERS: THE HEALTH INSURANCE MARKET FOR SMALL FIRMS

This research was supported
in part by the
Milbank Memorial Fund
and the
Russell M. Grossman Endowment

Size Matters: The Health Insurance Market for Small Firms

JILL MATHEWS YEGIAN, Ph.D.

Routledge
Taylor & Francis Group

LONDON AND NEW YORK

First published 1999 by Ashgate Publishing

Reissued 2018 by Routledge
2 Park Square, Milton Park, Abingdon, Oxon, OX14 4RN
52 Vanderbilt Avenue, New York, NY 10017

Routledge is an imprint of the Taylor & Francis Group, an informa business

Copyright © Jill Mathews Yegian, 1999

All rights reserved. No part of this book may be reprinted or reproduced or utilised in any form or by any electronic, mechanical, or other means, now known or hereafter invented, including photocopying and recording, or in any information storage or retrieval system, without permission in writing from the publishers.

Notice:
Product or corporate names may be trademarks or registered trademarks, and are used only for identification and explanation without intent to infringe.

Publisher's Note
The publisher has gone to great lengths to ensure the quality of this reprint but points out that some imperfections in the original copies may be apparent.

Disclaimer
The publisher has made every effort to trace copyright holders and welcomes correspondence from those they have been unable to contact.

A Library of Congress record exists under LC control number: 99072661

ISBN 13: 978-1-138-34287-3 (hbk)
ISBN 13: 978-0-429-43952-0 (ebk)

Contents

List of Figures and Charts

List of Tables

Introduction

Although the link between health insurance and employment in the United States was more an accident of history than an attempt to create an efficient system of coverage, it is now a firmly established connection. Given the importance of the connection between employment and health benefits, the role of the firm as a primary source of health care coverage merits close examination. The small firm, in particular, deserves attention: Small firms are much less likely to provide health care coverage to their employees, and many encounter significant difficulties obtaining coverage.

Each of the three chapters that comprise this work focuses on a different aspect of the health insurance market for small firms. First, an institutional economics perspective on the small group market for health insurance takes the view that the performance of the small firm as a purchaser is weak in comparison with large firms, but is susceptible to improvement. Explicating the source of the differential performance among firms of different sizes will allow public policy interventions to be more responsive to the underlying issues. Second, a history and political analysis of major regulatory reforms in the small group market for health insurance in California takes a case study approach to shed light on the interest group agendas and struggles that emerged in the process of legislative change. The potential effectiveness of public policy interventions is irrelevant if those interventions fail to emerge from the concept stage; the political analysis addresses the issue of feasibility of policy interventions at the level of state government. The third chapter presents an econometric analysis of the influence of premium and employer contribution on employee health plan choice in a purchasing cooperative setting for small firms. Although large firms have been studied extensively, small firms have received little attention; this project investigates choice behavior for employees of small firms.

A brief history and overview of the employment-based health insurance market in the United States — in general, and with a focus on small firms — provides context for the analyses to follow.

A Brief Historic Sketch[1]

During the nineteenth century, the key concern associated with illness was loss of income. Medical care had little curative ability, and hospitals were essentially places that poor sick people went to die (Starr 1982). Some voluntary associations, often occupation-related, formed groups that provided cash benefits to members who became sick and unable to work, but these groups generally did not cover medical care (Field and Shapiro 1993). With the evolution of biological understanding of disease and the development of more-effective treatments, people began to enter hospitals to be cured rather than to die. But no insurance against the catastrophic costs of treatment for major illness existed, and many were unable to pay their bills (Fein 1989).

Primarily as a way to create a steady flow of revenue, Baylor University Hospital in Texas created the precursor to Blue Cross in 1929 by establishing the first service benefit plan: In exchange for 50 cents a month, 1250 schoolteachers received up to 21 days of hospital care annually. From the beginning, employment groups presented attractive risk pools; they existed for reasons unrelated to medical care coverage, and were therefore not likely to be disproportionately comprised of high-risk individuals. The community-based, voluntary, nonprofit service benefit plans were popular, and Blue Cross grew rapidly. Hospital benefit plans were soon joined by Blue Shield plans providing physician service benefits. Commercial insurers at first avoided the market in the belief that medical care costs were inherently unpredictable. However, the success of Blue Cross plans, in conjunction with the desire of commercial insurers to offer consumers a complete array of insurance products, prompted their entry into the market during and after World War II (Fein 1989; Field and Shapiro 1993).

World War II wage policies resulted in a major expansion of employment-based health insurance. Fringe benefits, including health insurance, were exempted from the wartime wage freeze. The exemption provided a loophole through which employers could attract scarce labor by offering extensive health and other benefits in lieu of higher wages. Providing benefits, including health insurance, was particularly attractive because premiums and other costs were considered to be business expenses, and were therefore tax-deductible for employers. Another important factor was union activism in favor of the provision of health care benefits through the employment setting. Health care coverage continued to expand following the war, with the number of insured more than doubling between 1946 and 1951 (Fein 1989). By 1958, approximately 75 percent of the 123 million people with private medical care coverage obtained such coverage through employment (Field and Shapiro 1993).

Although most developed countries adopted or completed systems of comprehensive medical care provision or coverage for their citizens after World War II, the United States took a different path. The resulting system of voluntary employment-based health care coverage was not a foregone conclusion; national health insurance has been discussed in America since Theodore Roosevelt's 1912 proposal. The issue has re-emerged periodically, most recently with the discussion of President Clinton's proposal for national health care reform between 1992 and 1994. Although universal coverage will doubtless surface once again as an issue for serious nationwide consideration, the predominantly private, voluntary, employment-based system seems firmly entrenched for the present.

Overview of Employment-Based Coverage

In 1993, as Figure i.1 shows, employment-based coverage accounted for 59 percent of nonelderly health care coverage (Silverman et al. 1995 Table 8.1, p. 239).[2] Other sources were public insurance (Medicare, Medicaid, and CHAMPUS)[3] and other private insurance, such as individual policies. Seventeen percent of the nonelderly population was uninsured in 1993.

FIGURE I.1 Health Insurance Coverage of the Nonelderly, 1993

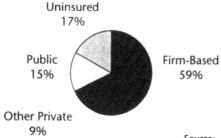

Uninsured
17%

Public
15%

Firm-Based
59%

Other Private
9%

Source: Silverman et al. (1995), Table 8.1, p. 239.

The firm has continued to play a major role in providing health care coverage to employees, but employment-based coverage has eroded somewhat in recent years. Between 1989 and 1993, the proportion of the population insured through employment dropped by five percentage points; some of those losing coverage through employment gained public insurance, but others joined the ranks of the uninsured (Silverman et al. 1995 Table 8.1, p. 239). A number of studies have shown that rates of employment-based coverage are slowly declining (Chollet 1994; Sullivan et al. 1992).

One reason is doubtless the inexorably rising costs of medical care. Health care expenditures in the U.S. have grown from 5.9 percent of gross domestic product (GDP) to 13.9 percent between 1965 and 1993, totaling $884.2 billion in 1993 (Silverman et al. 1995 Table 10.1, p. 346). During the same period, as Figure i.2 shows, employer expenditures on private health insurance grew from $5.9 billion to $235.6 billion; as a percent of total employee compensation, employer spending on health care grew from 1.5 percent to 7.3 percent between 1965 and 1993 (Silverman et al. 1995 Table 10.10, p. 364). The average annual rate of change for private health insurance expenditures between 1960 and 1994 was 12.5 percent (Health Care Financing Administration 1996 Table 1, p. 188). Cost growth has slowed somewhat in recent years, and employers experienced a 1.1 percent reduction in employer health costs in 1994 (Freudenheim 1995). However, the reduction was temporary, and costs began to rise again in 1995 (Freudenheim 1996).

FIGURE i.2   Employer Spending for Private Health Insurance, 1965-1993

Source: Silverman et al. (1995), EBRI Databook, Table 10.10, p. 364.

Health insurance coverage varies markedly with firm size. About three-quarters of uninsured individuals in this country are employed or the dependents of the employed, and of the uninsured employed, about half work in firms with fewer than 10 workers (Helms et al. 1992). As Figure i.3 shows, 60 percent of employees in firms with fewer than 10 workers were not offered health insurance, while only 5 percent of employees in firms with 250 or more workers were not offered coverage (Long and Marquis 1993).[4]

FIGURE I.3 Percent of Workers Not Offered Insurance, By Firm Size, 1988

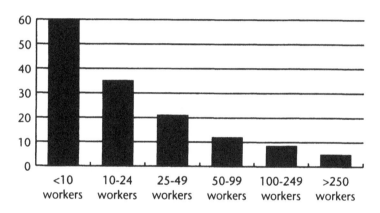

Source: Long and Marquis (1993), Exhibit 3, p. 286.

Thus, most of the uninsured work, and most of the working uninsured are employed in small firms. Why don't more small firms provide coverage? Table i.1, from a 1989 survey of small businesses, presents responses from employers not offering health care coverage to their employees. Small businesses cited high costs as the primary reason that coverage was not offered to employees (Hall and Kuder 1990), a finding that has been confirmed by a number of other surveys (Edwards et al. 1992; Health Insurance Association of America 1990; Helms et al. 1992; Jensen et al. 1993; Morrisey et al. 1994).

Indeed, health insurance is relatively more costly for small firms than it is for large firms. For the smallest employers, those with 1–4 workers, insurers charge an average of 40 percent of medical claims to cover administrative costs, including claims administration, commissions, risk, and profit.[5] That

TABLE I.1   Responses of Employers Not Providing Coverage

Reason for Not Offering Coverage	Percent of Employers Citing Reason
Premiums too high	65.3
Business insufficiently profitable	44.0
Employees covered elsewhere	42.8
Profits too unstable	39.1
Employees prefer cash/lack interest	34.1
Don't need insurance to attract good employees	22.5
Can't qualify for a group policy at group rates	22.2
Administrative expenses too high	16.5
Employee turnover too great	16.4
Other	6.8

Source: Hall and Kuder (1990), Table 7.24, p. 53.

figure decreases steadily with firm size: for the largest employers, those with 10,000 or more workers, insurers charge an average of only 5.5 percent of medical claims to cover administrative costs (Congressional Research Service, 1990, p. 12). Thorpe (1992) attributes the increased administrative costs for small groups to a higher failure rate for small businesses, increased employee turnover, and higher marketing and sales costs for small firms compared to larger firms.

The high cost of coverage is clearly the primary reason cited for not offering health benefits. But even when the costs are significantly reduced, few small employers choose to purchase coverage. With the objective of encouraging the development of innovative ways to expand coverage to small firms and individuals by reducing the cost, The Robert Wood Johnson Foundation launched a major initiative in 1986, the Health Care for the Uninsured Program. The ten funded projects took two main approaches: subsidization of coverage, and the development of new bare-bones insurance products that could be sold for significantly less than the more traditional generous policies (Helms et al. 1992). In addition, a Florida project created a purchasing cooperative for previously uninsured small firms. In spite of a significant reduction in premiums, either through subsidy or through the development of new lower-cost products, enrollment fell short of expectations. Premium discounts generally fell in the 25–50 percent range below market rates, but the lower rates failed to enroll more than a very small proportion of the target population of uninsured (Helms et al. 1992; McLaughlin and Zellers 1992). An evaluation of the program found that "there is a fairly hard-core group of small-business owners who do not want to provide health insurance benefits to their employees" (McLaughlin and Zellers 1992 p. 39).

Despite the high costs and other difficulties associated with obtaining and maintaining coverage, more small firms are offering insurance to their employees. Table i.2 shows the national trend in small-business coverage between 1989 and 1993, from survey data.

TABLE I.2 Percentage of Small Firms Offering Health Benefits, 1989-1993

No. of Employees	1989	1990	1991	1992	1993
1-9	32	27	25	41	44
10-24	71	72	55	54	70
25-49	89	85	77	83	85
All (1-49)	41	38	34	50	51

Source: Morrisey et al. (1994), Exhibit 1, p.151.

However, recent research has found that fewer employees are accepting the coverage offered by their employers (Cooper and Schone 1997). This finding was consistent across firms of all sizes, but was more pronounced in small firms than in large firms. The researchers offer several explanations for this phenomenon, including declining real incomes, the rising cost of coverage, and an increase in the share of health insurance premium costs paid by employees (compared to employers).

Although more surveys investigate the decision not to provide coverage, some data do exist on the choice of small employers to offer coverage. A 1989 survey of small businesses shows the percent of employers who offer coverage that answered affirmatively to reasons that they sponsor a health benefit plan. The most important reason cited was a perception that employees needed health care coverage (see Table i.3).

TABLE I.3   Responses of Employers Providing Coverage

Reason for Offering Coverage	Percent of Employers Citing Reason
Employees needed it	59.4
Boost employee morale	44.9
Good way to cover me/my family	43.5
Couldn't get/keep good employees without it	30.9
Employees asked for it	25.2
Plan in place before I took over	11.2
Cheaper than a wage increase	7.7
Union negotiation	4.5
A tragic event	1.1
Other	4.6

Source: Hall and Kuder (1990), Table 7.23, p. 52.

The Health Insurance Market for Small Firms

As long as insurance is voluntary, there will always be some firms that choose not to purchase coverage for their employees. However, taking the voluntary, employment-based insurance system currently in place as given, interventions in the small group market may improve its functioning for those firms interested in providing health care coverage. Although large firms are well suited to serving as the institution through which employees purchase benefits, small firms encounter difficulties in carrying out this role. Size enables large firms to reduce or eliminate two of the key problems that emerge as small firms attempt to cover their employees: (1) risk variability, which results in extensive underwriting of small firms, and (2) lack of economies of scale.

One measure with potential for improving the performance of the small firm as a purchaser of health care coverage is regulation to impose restrictions on the insurers that sell coverage to small firms. When the premiums that can be charged for health care coverage cannot vary based on the risk status of the small firm's employees, then employee-level risk assessment provides no benefit for the insurer. Regulation of the health insurance market for small firms can reduce the costs of coverage by reducing or eliminating the incentives for underwriting.

Another approach is to pool many small firms, creating purchasing alliances for health care coverage that can reduce risk variability and generate scale economies. Purchasing alliances present an alternative or a supplement to regulation. They mimic large firms by pooling many small firms into a larger entity for the purpose of purchasing health insurance. Joint purchasing increases negotiating ability and purchasing expertise for small firms, and expands health plan choice for small-firm employees. A cooperative can also serve as a centralized source of consumer information regarding health plan quality and cost-effectiveness. However, purchasing cooperatives can impose restrictions only on underwriting — thereby reducing or eliminating the cost of employee-level assessment — if the market outside the cooperative is also regulated. A close match between the internal rules of the pool and the rating structure outside the pool is critical to preventing debilitating adverse selection against the cooperative. If the pool features community rating and the market features unrestricted risk rating, the old and the sick will obtain a better deal inside the pool than they can outside. The predicted result is eventual collapse of the cooperative.

Chapter 1 applies the institutional economics literature to the issues of market structure and organizational form in the health insurance market for small firms, with particular attention to regulation and purchasing cooperatives as two forms of intervention. The chapter begins by tracing the development of the theoretical connection between quality variability and the market arrangements that arise to economize on costly information expenditures. The differential abilities of small and large firms to govern the health insurance transaction in a low-cost fashion are explicated. A neoclassical alternative to the employment-based health insurance system is briefly considered, but more attention is paid to market rules and purchasing cooperatives as mechanisms to improve the small firm's ability to purchase health insurance. A number of refutable implications that emerge from the analysis are explored, in part using information from a case study of California's approach to small-firm health insurance purchasing.

Regulation and purchasing cooperatives both have the potential to improve the health insurance market for small firms. But in the case of regulation, this potential cannot be realized without the political process. Even purchasing cooperatives, which can and do emerge as private entities, may be more likely to develop with the financial security and the credibility of government support. The creation of purchasing cooperatives encounters collective action obstacles; although all small firms might benefit, no small firm is interested in investing the required time and taking the financial risk. But is it realistic to expect the government to become involved in regulating the market and establishing purchasing cooperatives? What characterizes the state-level political process on health insurance issues related to small firms? Sparer (1994) has commented on a surprising lack of attention to state-level health care politics.

Regulation of insurers in the market for small firms appears unlikely considering the strong political influence of the insurance industry and the comparatively apolitical nature of entrepreneurs who are distracted by the day-to-day needs of running small businesses. Studying one state — California — that passed legislation in 1992 establishing both regulations and a purchasing cooperative for small firms is instructive. The new market rules include guaranteed issue and renewal of health care coverage, restricted premium levels, and limited the use of pre-existing condition exclusions. The legislation also created a voluntary alliance of small employers and assigned a state agency to serve as intermediary between the employers and health plans participating in the cooperative. The new purchasing cooperative was to provide extensive choice to the employees of small firms that joined and to allow small employers to access health care coverage at premiums generally available only to large firms.

Chapter 2 presents a detailed political history and analysis of California's 1992 reforms in the health insurance market for small firms, addressing both the new market rules and the purchasing cooperative, the Health Insurance Plan of California. The chapter begins with the context from which the reforms arose: the more general issue of access to health care coverage for the population at large. The analysis traces the shift in focus from providing universal coverage to improving access for one segment of the employment-based system: small firms. The chapter then characterizes the health insurance market for small firms, and describes the players, the issues, the proposals, and the outcome of the California debate. After briefly touching upon the failure of more comprehensive proposals, the discussion turns to the implementation of the measure. The major factors underlying the passage and implementation of the reforms are explored in detail.

If, as in California's case, a purchasing cooperative does become established through the political process, will small employers join? Will small employers that previously did not cover their employees join? What health plans will they choose, and will the plans chosen by previously insured employees differ from the plans chosen by previously uninsured employees? Chapter 3 describes the characteristics of the employees of small businesses that have joined California's purchasing cooperative, and explores the response of the employees to premium level and employer contribution in their choice of health plan. Although the influence of price on employee choice has been studied at some length in large-firm environments, small firms have received little attention to date. One major problem with studying this issue is that the majority of small firms that offer coverage to their employees provide only a single option (Morrisey et al. 1994). The purchasing cooperative that was included in California's reforms — the Health Insurance Plan of California — offers a broad selection of health plans to enrollees, and a rare opportunity to investigate employee-level choice among small firms.

To date, efforts to create a system of health care coverage that decouples insurance and employment have failed. At the same time, the importance of small firms in the U.S. economy has grown. Large firms have downsized, returning to their core competencies and outsourcing less central functions. Simultaneously, the rapid emergence of new industries, such as information technology, has generated growth in entrepreneurial start-up firms. While large firms employ the majority of the U.S. work force, small firms generate the majority of jobs (Headd, 1998). In 1995, firms with 1–99 workers comprised 85 percent of all firms; between 1990 and 1995, such firms created 63 percent of job growth in the U.S. (Acs et al. 1998, Figures 2 and 3).[6] In light of these figures, the issues that arise for small employers and their employees and dependents with respect to accessing health care coverage will only become more important. A thorough understanding of the dynamics of the health insurance market for small firms can contribute to the development of public policy interventions seeking to expand health care coverage for the employees of small firms.

Notes

1   This account is necessarily extremely brief. Starr (1982) provides an extensive historic account of the development of the institutions of American medicine, including health care coverage. For a historical explanation for the absence of national insurance in the United States, see Fein (1989).

2   Almost 100 percent of the elderly in the U.S. receive health care coverage through Medicare, a social insurance program that funds hospital insurance with payroll taxes and provides an optional supplementary insurance program that covers physician and other services.

3   In addition to providing coverage for the elderly, Medicare also covers nonelderly who are permanently disabled and those with kidney failure. Medicaid, the joint state and federal program, covers the poor who are also elderly, blind, or disabled, and poor single-parent families. CHAMPUS, the Civilian Health and Medical Program of the Uniformed Services, covers military dependents.

4   Not all of these employees are uninsured; other potential sources for coverage include a spouse's employment, public programs, or individual policies.

5   Further detail on level of administrative cost by firm size is provided in Table 2 of Chapter 1.

6   To measure job growth, firms are sorted by size and tracked over time. They remain in the same firm-size class for the measurement period, in this case 1990 to 1995, so that growth or contraction can be linked to firm size in Year 1 (1990). Other methods, such as using average employment for the measurement period (rather than Year 1 employment) to classify firm size, have also been used. See Headd (1998).

References

Acs, Z., Tarpley, F.A., and Phillips, B.D. (1998). *The New American Evolution: The Role and Impact of Small Firms.* Office of Economic Research, Office of Advocacy of the U.S. Small Business Administration, Washington, D.C.

Chollet, D. (1994). "Employer-Based Health Insurance In A Changing Work Force." *Health Affairs,* Spring (I), 315–326.

Congressional Research Service. (1990). *Private Health Insurance: Options for Reform.* U.S. Government Printing Office, Washington, D.C.

Cooper, P.F., and Schone, B.S. (1997). "More Offers, Fewer Takers For Employment-Based Health Insurance: 1987 And 1996." *Health Affairs,* November/December, 142–149.

Edwards, J.N., Blendon, R.J., Leitman, R., Morrison, E., Morrison, I., and Taylor, H. (1992). "Small Business and the National Health Care Reform Debate." *Health Affairs,* Spring, 164–173.

Fein, R. (1989). *Medical Care, Medical Costs.* Harvard University Press, Cambridge, Massachusetts.

Field, M.J., and Shapiro, H.T. (1993). "Employment and Health Benefits: A Connection at Risk." National Academy Press, Washington, D.C.

Freudenheim, M. (1995). "Health Costs Paid by Employers Drop for First Time in a Decade." *New York Times.* February 14. p. A1.

Freudenheim, M. (1996). "Health Costs for Workers in U.S. Rose Last Year, Reversing '94 Dip." *New York Times.* January 30. p. A1.

Hall, C.P., Jr., and Kuder, J.M. (1990). *Small Business and Health Care: Results of a Survey.* The NFIB Foundation, Washington, D.C.

Headd, B. (1998). *Small Business Growth by Major Industry, 1988–1995.* Office of Advocacy, U.S. Small Business Administration, Washington, D.C.

Health Care Financing Administration. (1996). *Health Care Financing Review,* Statistical Supplement.

Health Insurance Association of America. (1990). *Providing Employee Health Benefits: How Firms Differ.* Washington, D.C.

Helms, W.D., Gauthier, A.K., and Campion, D.M. (1992). "Mending The Flaws in the Small Group Market." *Health Affairs,* 11(2), 7–27.

Jensen, G.A., Morlock, R.J., and Gabel, J.R. (1993). "Small Businesses' Changing Views on Health Reform." *Journal of American Health Policy,* 3, 6–14.

Long, S.H., and Marquis, M.S. (1993). "Gaps in Employer Coverage: Lack of Supply or Lack of Demand?" *Health Affairs,* Supplement, 282–293.

McLaughlin, C.G., and Zellers, W.K. (1992). "The Shortcomings of Voluntarism in the Small Group Insurance Market." *Health Affairs,* Summer, 28–40.

Morrisey, M.A., Jensen, G.A., and Morlock, R.A. (1994). "Small Employers and the Health Insurance Market." *Health Affairs,* 13(5), 149–161.

Silverman, C., Anzick, M., Boyce, S., Campbell, S., McDonnell, K., Reilly, A., and Snider, S. (1995). *EBRI Databook on Employee Benefits.* Employee Benefit Research Institute, Washington, D.C.

Sparer, M.S. (1994). "The Unknown States." *The Politics of Health Care Reform: Lessons From the Past, Prospects for the Future,* J.A. Morone and G.S. Belkin, eds., Duke University Press, Durham, North Carolina, 430–439.

Starr, P. (1982). *The Social Transformation of American Medicine.* Basic Books, Inc., New York.

Sullivan, C.B., Miller, M., Feldman, R., and Dowd, B. (1992). "Employer-Sponsored Health Insurance in 1991." *Health Affairs,* 11(4), 172–185.

Thorpe, K.E. (1992). "Inside the Black Box of Administrative Costs." *Health Affairs,* Summer, 41–55.

1 The Small Firm as a Purchaser

Introduction

Although large firms are well suited to serving as the institution through which employees purchase benefits, small firms encounter difficulties in carrying out this role. Size enables large firms to reduce or eliminate two of the key problems that emerge as small firms attempt to cover their employees: risk variability, which results in extensive underwriting and associated high measurement costs in small firms, and lack of economies of scale. The objective of this analysis is twofold: first, to lay out the differences between small firms and large firms in their ability to effectively govern the health insurance transaction; and second, to assess mechanisms that can improve the performance of small firms. The mechanisms under consideration here are market rules and purchasing cooperatives.

As long as insurance is voluntary, there will always be some firms of all sizes that choose not to purchase coverage for their employees. Universal coverage, or even significant expansion of coverage, is unlikely without some form of compulsion. However, taking the private, voluntary, employment-based insurance system as given, reorganization of the small group market may improve its functioning for those firms interested in providing health care coverage.

Oliver Williamson's "discriminating alignment hypothesis," which forms the core of transaction cost economics, presents a conceptual lens for understanding the comparative advantages of different organizational forms in managing transactions: "transactions, which differ in their attributes, are aligned with governance structures, which differ in their cost and competence, so as to effect a discriminating — mainly, transaction cost economizing — result" (Williamson 1994 p. 14).[1,2] In this case, the transaction — purchase of health care coverage — does not vary, but the governance structures at issue here — large and small firms — differ substantially in their ability to manage the transaction. Thus, the focus is on delineating the "cost and competence" of governance structures with respect to the health insurance transaction.

Because small firms are less competent governance structures, mechanisms are more likely to arise to improve their performance than to aid large firms. Further, mechanisms differ in their performance-enhancing potential for small firms. Thus, the key objective is to perform a comparative analysis of alternative governance structures for the health insurance transaction.[3] Recognizing the difficulties associated with measuring transaction costs, Williamson emphasizes the comparative nature of the analysis: "[measurement] difficulties are significantly relieved by posing the issue of governance comparatively — whence the costs of one mode of governance are always examined in relation to alternative feasible modes" (Williamson 1994 p. 4).

Economists have tended to overemphasize the ability of prices to achieve efficiency in the health insurance market, and have endorsed "actuarial fairness" — premiums that reflect individual-level risk as fully as possible — to avoid incentive distortion (Cochrane 1995; Pauly 1970; Pupp 1981). Researchers from other disciplines have tended to perceive the proper function of health insurance as the redistribution of wealth from the healthy to the sick, advocating a single premium regardless of risk level — "moral fairness" — over risk-adjusted premiums (Daniels 1990; Stone 1993). This analysis takes neither of those paths. Instead, alternative modes of organizing the health insurance transaction are explored with neither a strict efficiency nor a redistributive agenda. Governance structures that economize on transaction costs or otherwise address costly features of the health insurance transaction are favored.

To establish a foundation for the firm as a governance structure for the health insurance transaction, section 2 traces the development of the theoretical connection between variability and the market arrangements that arise to economize on costly information expenditures. Section 3 differentiates between small and large firms in their ability to govern the health insurance transaction in a low-cost fashion. Section 4 briefly departs from employment-based health insurance to consider a neoclassical alternative. Section 5 returns to the firm as a governance structure, and considers market rules and purchasing cooperatives as mechanisms to improve the small firm's ability to purchase health insurance. Sections 6 and 7 compare the mechanisms, and evaluate implications that emerge from the analysis. Section 8 presents a case study of one state's approach to small-firm health insurance purchasing.

Variability, Information Asymmetry, and Differentiation

George Akerlof initiated discussion about the interaction between variability and asymmetric information with his 1970 paper on the used-car market. When sellers, but not buyers, can differentiate between items of varying quality, fewer (or no) trades will take place compared to the situation in which quality is obvious to both parties. This is because buyers, unable to differentiate, will offer average price for any given item. At that price, sellers with a high-quality item will be unwilling to sell and will exit the market. The average quality of the remaining items will now be lower, as will the price buyers are willing to offer. Again, the sellers with the highest-quality items among those remaining will be unwilling to sell. In the limit, only the "lemons" are left, and no trades will take place. As Table 1.1 demonstrates, Akerlof's classic example is analogous to the health insurance market. In the used-car market, the product is the used car, and uncertainty relates to the quality of the used car; in the health insurance market, the product is the risk level of the individual, and uncertainty relates to that risk level (not to the insurance policy itself).

But according to these scenarios, no used cars or health insurance policies would ever be traded. Since we know that both commodities are commonly exchanged, how do we reconcile this seemingly plausible story with real life? One approach is to note that although the quality of a used car and the risk of an individual may not be immediately obvious or observable, neither are they necessarily unknowable. Thus, buyers or sellers or both can spend resources to differentiate between "lemons" and "non-lemons" or between high risks and low risks. Such expenditures make information more symmetric and allow price to reflect extant variability.

Michael Spence (1973) developed the idea that, when they can gain from doing so, individuals will spend resources to differentiate themselves from others or from the average. Spence's model is as follows. Individuals will be paid for services in the labor market on the basis of average productivity even though they differ, because differentiating them is too costly for employers. The higher-productivity individuals will spend resources on

TABLE 1.1 Used Cars and High-Risk Individuals: Adverse Selection and "Lemons"

The Market for Used Cars	The Market for Individual Health Insurance
Buyers have incomplete information on the quality of used cars on the market	The insurer (buyer of risk) has incomplete information on the risk level of individuals seeking insurance
Sellers know the quality of their vehicles	Individuals know their own risk levels
Buyers offer an average price to all sellers, because they cannot differentiate between good and bad cars	The insurer offers an average premium ("community rating") to all sellers (individuals), because it cannot differentiate between low and high risks
Sellers with cars below the average price offer them for sale; other sellers exit the market	Sellers (individuals) with above-average risks accept the average premium; other individuals exit the market
The average quality of used cars on the market decreases, so the price offered by buyers drops	The average risk of individuals in the pool increases, so the premium charged by the insurer rises
Sellers with cars valued above the new (lower) average price exit the market	Individuals with risk below the new (higher) average exit the market
Eventually, only "lemons" are left, and no trades take place	Eventually, only "lemons" are left in the pool, and the premium offered by the insurer reflects their risk alone. They exit the pool as well, since they are paying insurer charges for profit and marketing as well as their own costs

higher education to differentiate themselves from the lower-productivity individuals, thereby earning higher-than-average wages. Their gain represents a loss to the other individuals, who now receive lower-than-average wages.[4]

Spence assumes that screening by the employer is more costly than signaling by the potential employee, so the latter takes place. But some employers spend significant resources to differentiate among prospective employees during intensive application and interview periods. Signaling by the potential employee and screening by the employer both allow price (wage) to more closely reflect variable productivity among employees. Likewise, incurring costs to differentiate between "lemons" and "non-lemons" used-car market and high and low risks in the health insurance market prevents the markets from unraveling by reducing the cross-subsidization that can result in market exit of the non-lemons and low risks. The result, if variability is fully differentiated, is that each car sells for its quality-adjusted value and that each insured pays the cost of his or her expected risk (plus loading fee) in premiums.

In the presence of quality variability and asymmetric information, spending resources on differentiation — up to the limit of cost-effectiveness — is relatively efficient, compared to allowing the market to unravel. But differentiation involves measurement costs, sometimes high costs. Yoram Barzel (1977) introduced the idea that constraints on differentiation expenditures can have economizing effects:

> Consider some people whose expected medical expenses are identical. Medical insurance, then, is sold to them at a uniform premium. With the progress of science, it is suddenly discovered that these expenses vary systematically across individuals. In a Spence-type world, we would now expect individuals who know that they are healthier to spend resources to convince insurance companies that they qualify for lower premiums. . . . The decline in premiums to healthier individuals will be accompanied by increases to all others. A redistribution of income from the sickly to the healthy, then, takes place at a positive resource cost (p. 302).

Barzel goes on to assert that, in spite of the potential for healthy individuals to gain at the expense of the sick, medical insurance is sometimes offered to groups (employees, union members, students). "A major feature of group health insurance is that no medical examination is required; individuals qualify simply by belonging to the group. Thus, a major sorting expense is bypassed" (p. 303). Barzel suggests that the reason that healthy individuals remain in the pooled group and submit to cross-subsidy to the sick is that eliminating the sorting expense that would otherwise be incurred creates substantial savings, such that purchasing inside the pool is less costly than purchasing outside the pool in spite of the cross-subsidy.

Building on Barzel, Roy Kenney and Benjamin Klein (1983) present three cases in which market mechanisms have emerged to prevent the costs that would have accompanied extensive differentiation: diamond sales by DeBeers, the distribution of motion pictures by Paramount and other major studios, and the sale of film rights to television. In each case, the seller set an average price for a product of heterogeneous quality (diamonds, films for theater, and films for television), and constrained the buyers' ability to spend resources to differentiate the highest-quality items from those of average and below-average quality. The outcome was significantly reduced buyer search and seller measurement costs.

Once one begins to look for differentiation costs and mechanisms to reduce such costs, they appear on all sides. In the used-car market, differentiation costs come in the form of paying a mechanic to check on the prospective purchase, an extensive array of publications (the most familiar of which is the "Blue Book"), and services that provide detailed estimates on the value of the car, given specific information on mileage and other relevant parameters (e.g., whether the car has power windows). Mechanisms to reduce differentiation costs include dealer-issued warranties that are less comprehensive than those for new cars but that still provide a significant degree of protection, and trading among friends and relatives (Barzel 1977). In the health insurance market, differentiation costs might include medical history questionnaires, physical exams, and laboratory tests; as noted by Barzel, one of the most important mechanisms to reduce underwriting costs is purchasing health insurance through a group.

Group-based insurance is prevalent in the United States, covering trade associations, unions, and especially firms. Employment-based insurance covers the vast majority of the insured under-65 population (Silverman et al. 1995).[5] To be sure, there are a number of reasons for the prevalence of employment-based insurance, including history and the tax code. A tradition of employment-based health insurance began during the World War II wage freeze; employers substituted fringe benefits, including health insurance, for prohibited wage increases. One powerful impetus for continuing the practice today is that insurance premiums paid by employers are tax deductible. But employment-based insurance would not likely endure without some cost-economizing feature of the sort observed by Barzel. The next section considers the firm as a governance structure for the health insurance transaction.

The Firm as a Governance Structure for the Health Insurance Transaction

Barzel's posited grouping mechanism for economizing on the health insurance transaction incorporates two assumptions, one explicitly and one implicitly. First, as asserted by Barzel, the well or low-risk members of the group must subsidize the sick or high-risk members. Second, Barzel implicitly assumes that the risk level of the group as a whole is sufficiently predictable to allow the insurer to forego assessment of individual members. Risk of individual group members can vary as long as the group as a whole presents a predictable risk profile, which depends on the size of the group. Costly differentiation can take place on either side of the transaction: Healthy group members can distinguish themselves from the sick to obtain lower premiums, insurers can individually screen the members of prospective groups, or both types of activities can occur. Some degree of economizing on the transaction can occur if either or both sides consent to reduce differentiation activities. Consider each side in turn.

Why do low-risk employees consent to redistribution to high-risk employees? Perhaps the most important reason is that employers most often offer employees a choice between health benefits and no health benefits, not between health benefits and some other benefit or additional take-home pay. Some employers do offer such "cafeteria" packages, but they are in the minority.[6] Thus, low-risk employees can either accept the offered benefits, which incorporate the subsidy to higher-risk employees, or decline them without alternative compensation.

In those cases in which employers do allow employees to trade health benefits for other benefits or cash, one might expect that low-risk employees would accept the alternative compensation and purchase health care coverage on the market. A low-risk employee who considers purchasing coverage as an individual will receive a discount in the individual market, which differentiates among individuals based on risk. But the tax-deductibility of employer contributions to employee premiums creates an incentive for the employee to obtain coverage inside the firm: Employer contributions to employee premiums are not taxed, while coverage outside the firm must be purchased with after-tax dollars. The individual's risk-based discount must offset not just the tax-deductible employer contribution but also the administrative hassles and the lack of economies of scale experienced by an individual purchasing on the open market.

The second requirement for the firm as an effective group purchasing mechanism is that buyers of risk — insurers — forego differentiating among risk levels. Insurers will be willing to forego individual assessment of the employees as long as the firm as a whole provides a predictable level of risk.

Here, the size of the firm comes into play. Risk predictability falls on a spectrum — most predictable in the largest groups and least predictable in the smallest. The point on the spectrum at which insurers are willing to forego individual assessment in favor of group assessment varies from insurer to insurer, but the smallest firms are always assessed individually while the largest firms are always assessed as a single unit.

The next section elaborates on the differential capacity of small and large firms to serve as governance structures for the health insurance transaction. Because risk is much more variable in small firms than in large, the costs of differentiating risk levels through underwriting and screening at renewal are much higher in small firms. In addition, large firms possess scale advantages in the provision of health care coverage; in addition to lower administrative costs, larger firms feature greater purchasing sophistication and a wider selection of health insurance options for employees.

Risk Variability

Large firms transform unpredictable individual-level risk into predictable group-level risk by pooling a large number of individuals. Intuitively, this makes sense: As a group grows, the insurer's ability to estimate losses improves. The law of large numbers, which is frequently cited as the statistical mechanism underlying insurance, can be summarized as follows: "Under this law, the impossibility of predicting a happening in an individual case is replaced by the demonstrable ability to forecast collective losses from a large number of cases" (Mehr 1986 p. 39). Figure 1.1 depicts the relationship between firm size and risk predictability. The 1000-employee firm has a much tighter distribution, with a much lower variance, than does the 10-employee firm, even though they have the same expected health care expenditures. From the graph, it is obvious that health care costs for the small firm are much more likely to fall far from their expected value than are health care costs for the large firm. For a mathematical example of the connection between firm size and risk variability, refer to the Appendix.

The link between firm size and risk variability demonstrates that insurers will be unable to predict losses as accurately for small firms as for large firms, implying that insurers will be more likely to invest, and to invest more, in measuring the risk levels in small firms than in large firms. The next section describes some of the activities undertaken to differentiate

FIGURE 1.1 The Relationship Between Firm Size and Risk Predictability

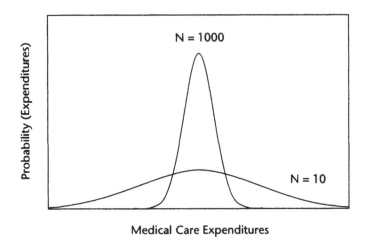

Medical Care Expenditures

risk in small firms, and compares those activities to large-firm risk differentiation.

Differentiation Costs in Small Firms

Before describing the costs associated with risk differentiation in small firms, brief mention is made of the "burning house syndrome," a form of adverse selection that increases the incentive for insurers to carefully evaluate the risk of small firms.

Burning House Syndrome "Burning house syndrome" is named for those who attempt to purchase fire insurance while their houses burn down. In employment-based insurance, this phenomenon may arise when the employment group is small enough for an individual to seriously impact or actually make the decision to purchase insurance based on his or her needs or preferences (e.g., a business owner with three employees needs medical care and so applies for insurance for the whole group). One common case is the family-owned business, in which many or all of the employees are members of the same family. "A minimum of, say, 10 or 25 persons gives the insurer some protection against the insurance being taken primarily out for the purpose of covering one or more individuals with incipient losses and claims" (Gregg 1973 p. 356). By contrast, the decision to obtain and maintain health benefits for a firm of 1000 employees will be made based on business considerations — the benefit package that is needed to attract labor, the financial profile of the firm, and like factors — rather than on the health status of the CEO. Of course, individual employees may move in and out of a firm as their needs for health benefits wax and wane. Although this doubtless occurs, it seems unlikely that a significant number of people observe an upcoming need for medical care, find an employment position with health benefits, and then depart the job when the episode is complete, only to repeat the cycle when the need for further care is anticipated.

The burning house phenomenon may be the result of ignorance or strategizing on the part of the insured; what matters to the insurer is the incidence of adverse selection, not its rationale. Regardless of the reason, the fact of its existence increases the importance of careful assessment of small-employer applicants to weed out those who apply for insurance in response to an immediate need for benefits.

Underwriting   "Underwriting is the process of accepting or rejecting risks (prospective insureds). If a risk is accepted, underwriting is further concerned with the terms under which the particular risk is insured" (Mehr et al. 1985 p. 635). This statement implies several stages: screening applicants, deciding whether to accept or reject, and classifying the accepted applicants into relatively homogeneous risk categories. The more thorough the underwriting, the more homogeneous the risk categories (the less risk variability within each risk group), the more accurately premiums can reflect risk, and the more costly the measurement process.

In the smallest firms, employees are evaluated individually. The threshold for individual assessment is not fixed; common figures in the literature include 10, 15, and 25 employees (Congressional Research Service 1988; Congressional Research Service 1990; Thomas 1973; Trapnell 1990). Evidence of insurability is virtually always required in the individual market; at a minimum, prospective enrollees detail their medical histories and personal information on the application for coverage. According to a 1987 Office of Technology Assessment survey of insurers, the key underwriting factors in evaluating applicants were age, occupation, health habits (*e.g.*, smoking, drug abuse), and illegal or unethical behavior.[7] Also important were avocation (*e.g.*, race car driving) and financial status (Eden et al. 1988 p. 15, Table 8). When the application provided information that required further investigation for underwriting, the insurers used one or more of the following: attending physician statements, physical exams, blood or urine screening, and financial or personal investigation (Eden et al. 1988 p. 24, Table 15).

The insurers who responded to the survey classified 73 percent of applicants as standard, 20 percent as substandard, and 8 percent as uninsurable. Substandard classification signifies a higher premium, exclusion of a condition from coverage, or both. The exclusion can be temporary or permanent, and can apply narrowly to a condition or broadly to an organ system. Temporary exclusions tend to be for acute conditions that are expected to resolve quickly, while permanent exclusions generally apply to chronic conditions that will incur significant costs over a long period of time. Conditions that often result in higher premiums include arthritis, back strain, controlled hypertension, and glaucoma. Conditions that may cause exclusion waivers include cataracts, hernias, migraine headaches, allergies, or asthma. Emphysema, severe obesity, alcoholism, cancer, and AIDS were among the reasons that insurers refused to issue policies (Eden et al. 1988 p. 15, Table 8).

Zellers et al. (1992) found that small-group-market insurers consistently required a detailed personal and family medical history from all applicants, and sometimes also mandated a physical exam. The survey found frequent exclusion of entire industries that are perceived to be at comparatively high risk for medical expenditures: "those characterized by an older work force (over age 55) or high employee turnover, those engaged in seasonal work or exposed to hazardous working conditions, those lacking an employer/employee relationship, and those 'known to present frequent claims submissions'" (p. 174). Industries most frequently mentioned as ineligible included physician groups (high utilizers), law firms (litigious), and hair salons (high turnover, a high proportion of women of childbearing age, and a high proportion of gay men).

A survey of employers, consisting of more than 22,000 telephone interviews with firms of various sizes in ten different states, found that the smallest firms were much more likely to be medically underwritten than larger firms (Cantor et al. 1995 Exhibit 6). Forty-two percent of firms with 1–4 employees reported medical underwriting, with steadily decreasing figures for firms with 5–9, 10–24, and 25–49 employees. Of the largest firm size in the study, 50 or more employees, 21 percent of respondents reported under-writing. In presenting the survey results, the authors group all firms with 50 or more employees into one category; the extent of underwriting in larger firms — those with 500 or 1000 employees, which presumably have little or no underwriting — cannot be distinguished.

Screening at Renewal   The initial underwriting process, providing the basis for the first-year's premiums, is the most intensive. However, renewal rating may also involve screening, usually reviewing the claims from the past year to see whether they are in line with expected costs. Insurers may respond to adverse claims experience by canceling the policy at renewal time or renew-ing the policy but excluding the individuals responsible for the expendi-tures. More often, premiums will be updated at renewal. Two rating structures are commonly used in the small group market. Durational rating is less costly in a measurement sense than is tier rating, because the latter requires a reassessment of the group's risk.

Durational rating, also called select and ultimate rating, features sepa-rate rate tables based on time with the current insurer (Congressional Research Service 1990; Hall 1992; Trapnell 1990). There may be just two rate tables, one for policyholders in their first year and one for all other policy-holders (hence the terms select and ultimate). Or there may be tables for each year up to, for example, year five, at which time all policyholders are combined into one risk pool (Trapnell 1990 p. 23). One large California insurer uses the two-table form of durational rating for its small group busi-ness: It assigns premiums based on a "newness" rate table for groups in their first year and a different rate table for all subsequent years. New groups receive a discount of approximately 8 percent. The rationale behind the con-sistently climbing rates is that time erodes the effects of the initial under-writing activities. Although high-risk group members may have been excluded at the outset, group members who were initially healthy develop costly medical conditions over time. Additionally, pre-existing condition exclusions expire (assuming they were temporary rather than permanent).

In durational rating, the movement from one rate table to the next is automatic, based solely on the passage of time. Thus, no additional screen-ing need be undertaken for renewals. This is not the case with tiered rating, which takes into account the claims experience of the group over the prior time period. "The insurer will investigate each enrollee within a group who incurred high medical costs and attempt to judge whether the same enrollee will continue to be costly in the future. On the basis of this assessment, the group will then be assigned to a rate 'tier,' one of an ascending series of rate levels. The rate for a high tier may be as much as 200 to 400 percent of the insurer's average premium for small groups" (Congressional Research Service 1990 p. 13).

In a variation on durational rating, insurers sometimes give employers the option of proving that they are still a good risk, allowing them to return to the low rates of new policyholders if they are able to do so. The Congressional Research Service study (1988 p. 37) quotes an insurer discussing rating practices for small firms:

> We have chosen to durationally rate the business. That is, as business ages, rates increase over the new business rates. At a select point in time, though, we give the groups an opportunity to reenter. If the group provides us with new evidence of insurability, it reverts to the new business rate. This forces a selection between bad business and good business. We keep the healthy groups that otherwise would leave and we isolate and concentrate our resources on watching the bad business. Bad business is isolated from the rest of the business, so we can take renewal action on it as needed.

This form of rating is closer to tiered rating, in the sense that it requires screening activities.

Insurer rating practices and employer desire for low rates interact to produce a high turnover between small employer and insurer. When an employer first signs on, the firm often receives low rates both because the insurer is attempting to attract new business and because the insurer is protected by initial screening activities. When the exclusions expire and/or one or more employees need medical care, rates can increase steeply. This can send employers back out to the market in search of a new insurer, starting the cycle of risk assessment and measurement costs over again.

Differentiation Costs in Large Firms

Because underwriting is not perceived to be a problem for large firms, much less research has been performed on the extent of risk differentiation activities. Although some have asserted that underwriting of large firms is more widespread than is generally perceived (Stone 1993), there is little argument that such activities are much more common in small firms than in large firms. An employee beginning a new job at a large firm is usually not required to fill out health questionnaires and submit medical records as a condition of obtaining coverage. One caveat applies to employees who initially decide not to enroll in the employer-sponsored coverage program, and then later apply for coverage. This behavior signals the insurer that circumstances have changed for the employee in a way that makes insurance desirable, and insurers will often require evidence of insurability under these conditions (Eden et al. 1988; Thomas 1973).[8]

Insurer screening costs are low in large firms because insurers need not invest resources in estimating risk on an individual basis. Predictability of risk renders individual-level assessment unnecessary; with large firms, the insurer can simply experience-rate the firm, meaning that the firm's premium is directly related to its costs during the previous year. Firms with a sufficiently large employee base benefit from the compression of risk variability to the point at which year-to-year fluctuations disappear. Pure experience rating, which amounts to a retrospective adjustment each year to account for the expenses incurred during the prior year, is the lowest-cost method of rating large firms because it completely eliminates individual-level assessment.

It may seem as though firms could dispense with insurers altogether when they become large enough that their health risks were predictable. In fact, many firms have decided to self-insure[9] — to internalize the health insurance transaction by assuming the risk for their employees, rather than passing it onto an insurer. Large firms can save by self-financing; the firms themselves — rather than insurers — can earn returns on invested premiums, paying employee medical costs as they arise. However, since removing a transaction from the market and internalizing it is a last resort (Williamson 1979; Williamson 1991), we might expect that some other factor is influencing the decision to self-insure. The primary factor is the Employee Retirement and Income Security Act of 1974 (ERISA). Under ERISA, self-insuring firms are exempt from state regulation of insurance companies, most important, state-mandated benefits and state premium taxes.[10] By self-insuring rather than purchasing insurance, firms can also escape levies on insurance companies that are passed on through premiums. For example, many states have created high-risk pools for "uninsurable" individuals and require insurers to help subsidize premiums.

Overall, about 40 percent of all employees are enrolled in self-insured health plans (Sullivan et al. 1992). As might be expected from risk predictability considerations, larger firms are much more likely to self-insure than are smaller firms; survey data from 1991 and 1993 estimate that approximately 10 percent of insured workers in firms with fewer than 100 employees are enrolled in self-insured plans, while approximately 60 percent of insured workers in firms with 500 or more employees are enrolled in self-insured plans (Acs et al. 1996 Exhibit 1). Thus, higher-risk variability results not just in higher underwriting costs for small firms but also in higher costs associated with fully insuring (rather than self-insuring), including state-mandated benefits and premium taxes.

Economies of Scale

The term "economies of scale" is used loosely here to refer to features associated with size rather than to specifically indicate increasing technological returns to scale. There are three sources of economies of scale in the health insurance transaction: administrative costs associated with contracting, underwriting, and claims; sophistication and expertise in purchasing, given the complexity of the health insurance market; and choice among health care coverage options.

Administrative Costs

An insurance textbook characterizes group insurance as "essentially low-cost mass protection. A number of economies of large volume operation are obtained through mass distribution and mass administration methods" (Gregg 1973 p. 353). Table 1.2 supports that assertion, and links the extent of the economies to the size of the group.

Figures from the Congressional Research Service (1990), estimated by Hay-Huggins, provide evidence that health insurance is relatively more costly for small firms than it is for large firms in a number of areas. Small firms pay more than do large firms in every category; the most dramatic difference is in the "General Administration" category. General Administration includes the costs of assessing and pricing out risk (underwriting) that were discussed in the last section; also included are the costs of advertising, billing, and general operating overhead. For the smallest employers, those

TABLE 1.2   Administrative Expenses, as Percentage of Incurred Claims

Number of Employees	Claims Adminis-tration	General Adminis-tration	Profit and Risk	Com-mission	Interest Credit	Premium Taxes	Total
1 to 4	9.3	12.5	8.5	8.4	–1.5	2.8	40.0
5 to 9	8.6	11.2	8.0	6.0	–1.5	2.7	35.0
10 to 19	7.2	9.2	7.5	5.0	–1.5	2.6	30.0
20 to 49	6.3	7.6	6.8	3.3	–1.5	2.5	25.0
50 to 99	4.3	4.8	6.0	2.0	–1.5	2.4	18.0
100 to 499	4.1	4.0	5.5	1.6	–1.5	2.3	16.0
500 to 2,499	3.9	3.2	3.5	0.7	–1.5	2.2	12.0
2,500 to 9,999	3.8	1.4	1.8	0.3	–1.5	2.2	8.0
10,000 or more	3.0	0.7	1.1	0.1	–1.5	2.1	5.5

Source: Congressional Research Service (1990), p. 12.

with 1–4 workers, insurers charge an average of 12.5 percent of claims to cover general administration. For the largest employers, those with 10,000 or more workers, insurers add 0.7 percent to claims to cover general administration. The grand total for the smallest employers is 40 percent of medical claims, compared to 5.5 percent for the largest employers.

Expertise

The market for health insurance is both complex and rapidly changing, and small firms are ill-suited to evaluating the available options and making informed decisions. Insurance agents and brokers can provide much-needed help. But such intermediaries are compensated by the insurance companies and health plans, not by the small firms. Thus, they are necessarily influenced by economic incentives unrelated to the needs of small businesses, such as the commission and bonus structures of insurers. Large firms, by contrast, generally maintain benefits departments and often hire consultants to supplement internal expertise.

Williamson (1995) notes that participants in intermediate product markets tend to be relatively well informed compared to participants in final

product markets: ". . . many final consumer . . . transactions are characterized by (comparatively) shallow knowledge, confusion, inability to craft a
specialized governance structure, weak reputation effects and costly legal
processes" (p. 39). This distinction aptly describes the difference between
large and small firms in the health insurance market. Large employers function as though health care coverage for their employees is one of many
intermediate products that they purchase in the process of producing goods
or services, while small employers are likely to act much more like individuals purchasing coverage in the retail market.[11]

Choice

The majority of small firms that provide insurance to their employees offer
only one coverage option. Survey data reveal that only 2 percent of firms
with fewer than 50 workers offer two or more health plans (Morrisey et al.
1994). The majority of small firms offering coverage provide fee-for-service
insurance, which tends to be more costly than managed care plans. Almost
60 percent of firms with fewer than 50 workers offered a single fee-for service
plan, while 6 percent offered an HMO and 10 percent offered a PPO (Morrisey et al. 1994 p. 152, Exhibit 2). Large firms are more likely to offer a
choice, and to include more affordable managed care plans among the
health care coverage options.

Comparative Assessment of Small and Large Firms as Governance Structures

Risk variability and scale features make large firms much more effective governance structures for the health insurance transaction than are small firms.
Not coincidentally, the percentage of firms that provide health insurance
increases consistently with firm size, with by far the largest percentage of
uninsured firms in the smallest size categories (Long and Marquis 1993;
Silverman et al. 1995 Table 8.12). Large firms enjoy advantages over small
firms in all five of the respects discusssed above: measurement costs associated with underwriting, measurement costs associated with renewal screening, administrative costs, expertise and sophistication in purchasing, and
availability of employee choice of health plan.

Based on the shortcomings of small firms in managing the health insurance transaction, one might conclude that the small firm is an ineffective mode of providing health insurance and that small firms should abandon the health care coverage function. Alternatively, one could search for ways to improve the performance of the small firm as a governance structure, so that it more closely matches the performance of the large firm. Each of these responses to the demonstration of differential performance of small and large firms in the health insurance market is explored below.

Neoclassical Approach: Contracts and Lump Sum Transfers

Many economists see little advantage in employment-based health insurance, even through the relatively efficient governance structure of the large firm. Arrow, in his classic article on the economics of medical care, put forth the efficiency perspective of economists with respect to risk rating: "Hypothetically, insurance requires for its full social benefit a maximum possible discrimination of risk. Those in groups of higher incidences should pay higher premiums" (1963 pp. 963–4). Not only does employment-based health insurance incorporate redistribution from the healthy to the sickly but the tax-deductibility of employer contributions that keep the healthy in the firm-based pool also distort incentives. Consistent with the traditional analytic distinction between efficiency and equity, neoclassical economists tend to favor full risk rating, so that "non-discriminatory prices that equal the cost of providing goods and services to each individual will be charged" (Pupp 1981 p. 611).

This section briefly considers one proposal for an alternative to employment-based health insurance. Consistent with the efficiency emphasis of neoclassical economists, the proposal emphasizes differentiation between the well and the sick, with premiums reflecting health status. The key innovation is "time-consistent health insurance," a contractual solution to the year-to-year fluctuations in risk that are inevitable whenever individual insurance replaces group-based insurance (Cochrane 1995). The same issue — a desire for protection against the possibility of a decline in health status from one period to next — has gained attention among other economists as well, who have used the terms "risk redefinition" (Dowd and Feldman 1992 p. 148) and "risk of becoming a high risk" (Pauly 1992 p. 140) to describe the problem.

The essence of Cochrane's proposal is as follows:

> . . . each consumer has a special account that can be used only to pay health insurance premiums and pay or receive severance payments. Every period, the consumer pays a constant amount into the account, and the account pays a premium to an insurer for one-period insurance. Competition requires that sick people pay higher premiums and healthy people pay lower premiums. If a person is diagnosed with a disease that raises his premiums, the insurer pays into the account a lump sum equal to the increase in the present value of premiums. If he gets healthier so that his premiums decline, the account pays the insurer a lump sum equal to the decline in the present value of premiums. (p. 448)

Given that premiums are updated each period to reflect expected costs for the prior period, it is not clear how this scheme is different from a savings plan. John Cochrane differentiates medical savings accounts (MSAs) from his proposal by asserting that MSAs pay for services while his proposal pays insurance premiums. But if insurance premiums reflect the expected costs of each individual and are regularly updated, is this a meaningful distinction? And does the proposal really meet the needs of the individual wishing to protect against a future change in health status? The insurer, according to the proposal, pays the account in the event that the individual experiences a decline in health status. How would the contract be enforced, particularly if the decline were so severe as to warrant a large payout by the insurer?

Without delving deeply into the details of this contractual scheme, it appears to feature high transaction costs and to ignore bounded rationality and incomplete contracting (Williamson 1985). Cochrane, anticipating objections to the proposal based on difficulties with calculating the transfer amounts, asserts that "time-consistent contracts do not require a difficult and possibly contentious computation of expected health expenses" (p. 459). But it is unclear how the present value of future premiums can be easily and uncontroversially calculated to ensure that transfers flow seamlessly between the account and the insurer. Particularly relevant for these calculations are rising medical care costs and rapid changes in technology. Much innovative medical technology is cost-increasing (Schwartz 1994) as well as lifesaving, posing clear difficulties for the calculation of transfer amounts. But Cochrane dismisses this issue: "Technology does not automatically raise costs. Almost by definition, improvements in technology imply declines in the price of treatment. When a cure for a previously untreatable disease is discovered, the price declines from infinity to some possibly large value" (p. 464).

Cochrane's equations describe the terms for "Pareto-optimal, time-consistent health insurance contracts" (p. 468), based on numerous assumptions. But showing mathematically that a contractual solution could theoretically improve the functioning of the health insurance market falls short of providing a viable alternative to the current employment-based system. The next section considers two alternatives that take the employment-based system as given, and pursue different directions to build on it.

Mechanisms for Improving on the Small Firm as a Governance Structure

Given the entrenchment of the employment-based system of health care coverage that prevails in the U.S., improving the performance of the small firm as a governance structure for the health insurance transaction merits consideration. Two approaches are considered below. One approach — market rules — derives from a market failure orientation. The other — purchasing cooperatives — attempts to operationalize lessons from the successful governance of the health insurance transaction by large firms.

Market Failure Approach: Market Rules Restrict Rating

One approach to small firm difficulties managing the health insurance transaction has been to regulate insurers in order to eliminate some of the behaviors perceived to be causing problems, particularly underwriting and screening at renewal. By contrast with the neoclassical emphasis on full risk rating, the advocates of the market failure approach believe that unlimited risk rating in the market for small firms results in lack of access for some small firms who are denied coverage, and effective lack of access for others that are offered coverage only at prohibitive premiums that reflect their risky health status. Underlying the access problems is the inability of small firms to internalize the compression of risk variance. The proposed solution has been to enact legislation that prohibits insurers from allowing premiums to fully reflect risk variability. A market failure perspective dictates this approach: Government intervention is the appropriate response to right the wrongs of the small-firm market. Because the employers experiencing the greatest difficulties with access and affordability are those at high risk, the market rules incorporate an element of redistribution from low-risk to high-risk small firms. But by restricting variation in premiums, the market rules also reduce the cost of differentiating between the high- and low-risk firms.

For the purposes of this discussion, rating restrictions are the key element of the market rules because of the role they play in reducing the costs of differentiating among small firms. But before addressing rating methods and their ramifications, the other market rules merit brief note. Guaranteed issue requires that insurers selling policies to any small employer must sell policies to all interested small employers; neither groups nor members of groups can be denied coverage.[12] Guaranteed renewal prohibits insurers from canceling policies for any reason other than fraud, nonpayment of premiums, or failure to meet the terms of the contract.[13] Continuity of coverage limits the application of pre-existing condition exclusions. Rather than repeated exclusion of pre-existing conditions every time an individual changes insurers or plans, continuity of coverage restricts exclusions to a single lifetime limit of a specified number of months, as long as the individual is continuously insured. The non-rating components of the market rules, particularly guaranteed issue and renewal, are essential to achieving the access objective — without guaranteed issue and renewal, insurers can deny coverage to high-risk small firms, or drop coverage after the first period. However, since rating restrictions are of primary interest for this discussion, we will assume that guaranteed issue and renewal exist and are held constant across different rating schemes without further elaboration. The discussion now turns to three rating methods: pure community rating, community rating by class, and full risk rating.

Under a pure community rating scheme, rates vary only according to family status (single or family coverage), geographical area, and plan or benefit design (American Academy of Actuaries 1993). Other factors, including age, sex, occupation, and health status cannot affect premium. Thus, the insurer receives the same amount of money for each subscriber (in the same region, family status, and plan), regardless of risk level. Under a pure community rating system, the healthy subsidize the sick, the young subsidize the old, those in low-risk occupations subsidize those in high-risk occupations, and so forth.

Community rating by class is distinguished from pure community rating by additional adjustments for select demographic factors, or "classes," most often age and sex (American Academy of Actuaries 1993). Community rating by class eliminates the subsidy for the factors included as adjusters. Thus, if age and sex are the classes, the elderly and women of childbearing age no longer receive subsidies. However, cross-subsidies for factors affecting risk but not included as classes remain in the system, including the subsidy for health status — the well still subsidize the sick.

Full risk rating signifies that the premium fully reflects the risk status of the individual or group. Thus, in addition to the adjustments for geographical area and family status of pure community rating and the age and sex adjustments of community rating by class, full risk rating might include rate modifications for occupation, past claims experience, diagnoses, habits (e.g., smoking), and any other factor that can be ascertained by the insurer and related to risk of health expenditures.

Trade-offs among these methods of rating have motivated voluminous discourse, much of it relating to the struggle between the "actuarial fairness" of full risk rating and the "moral fairness" of pure community rating.[14] Putting aside the redistribution issue, the focus here is on the potential of each rating method to reduce differentiation costs without creating incentives for low-risk firms to exit the market, which could result in the unraveling market phenomenon discussed early in this chapter.

Pure community rating reduces differentiation costs for insurers because there is no incentive to investigate the risk level of an individual firm. Ascertaining any information other than geographic area and family status is costly, and the results cannot be reflected in the premium. Similarly, community rating by class entails very low differentiation costs because underwriting at the individual level yields no benefits. The usual adjustment factors, age and sex, are unambiguous and simple to assess. By contrast, full risk rating encourages insurers to differentiate among policy applicants as completely as possible. Insurers that do not fully differentiate will not be able to offer the lowest possible premium to the lowest-risk small firms because their rates will include cross-subsidy to higher-risk firms. The low-risk firms will then seek out the insurers that have managed to differentiate risk more fully, creating an incentive for all insurers to spend resources to sort firms on risk as thoroughly as possible.

Under any significant departure from full risk rating, and particularly under pure community rating, some of the lowest-risk firms can be expected to weigh the increase in premiums against the value of their coverage. Some may exit the market. Prices will then rise for the remaining groups, whose average costs are higher now that some of the lowest-cost firms have left. A cycle of exit by low-risk firms followed by an increase in premium for the remaining firms can result. Whether this "death spiral" actually occurs depends on a number of factors, including the restrictiveness of the rating system, the competitiveness of the market (competition will help keep the price increases down for the low-risk firms), and the price elasticity of demand for insurance among small firms. A key deciding factor is whether low-risk small firms have other coverage options that retain their health status discount. If the market for small firms becomes community rated while the individual market remains fully risk rated, low-risk small employers will have an incentive to drop the group policy and instead purchase discounted individual policies. However, if the individual market is also community rated, the employer cannot obtain a risk-related discount in either market. In this case, exiting the market entails exposure to possibly catastrophic medical costs.

The relevant features of the three rating methods are displayed in Table 1.3. It is assumed that the individual market remains fully risk rated, allowing low-risk small employers exiting the small group market to obtain discounts in the individual market. While pure community rating features low differentiation costs, it encourages the exit of low-risk small employers. Full risk rating, which resolves market stability problems, features high differentiation costs associated with underwriting small firms at the individual level. Community rating by class provides an intermediate position.

The table implies that government intervention to establish market rules has the potential to reduce differentiation costs, and that community rating by class is preferable to pure community rating.

TABLE 1.3   Features of Rating Methods

	Pure Community Rating	Community Rating By Class	Full Risk Rating
Differentiation Costs	Low	Low	High
Incentive for Low-Risk Exit	High	Low/Moderate	Low

Pooling Small Firms: Lessons from Large Firms

Regulation provides one approach to restructuring the small group market; formation of purchasing cooperatives provides another. The success of large firms in governing the health insurance transaction has not gone unnoticed, and purchasing cooperatives mimic large firms by pooling many small firms into a larger entity for the purpose of purchasing health insurance. Pooling small firms is not a new concept: Multiple Employer Welfare Arrangements (MEWAs) and Multiple Employer Trusts (METs) have long provided health insurance to groups of small firms. However, although METs and MEWAs do pool small firms, the term "purchasing cooperative" is something of a misnomer for these entities because they are generally operated by insurers rather than by a purchaser advocate. Confusion over regulatory authority and the shady dealings of some MEWAs have gained these organizations a reputation for bankruptcy, abrupt termination of coverage, and outright fraud (General Accounting Office 1992; Long 1992; Tuller 1989).[15]

The current generation of purchasing cooperatives is generally more than simply enlarged risk pools run by insurance companies. Usually structured to act as agents of enrolled employers, they provide scale economies that are lacking in small firms and that market rules alone do not generate. Recall that relevant measures of scale economies are broadly defined for the purpose of this analysis as three areas in which large firms have a clear advantage over small firms with respect to the health insurance transaction: administrative costs, purchasing expertise, and choice of health plan. Purchasing cooperatives provide an advantage over market rules in two of the three: purchasing expertise and choice. Joint purchasing allows for much greater purchasing sophistication than would be possible for any small firm negotiating independently, and it expands health plan choice for small-firm employees. In addition, a cooperative can serve as a centralized source of consumer information regarding health plan quality and cost-effectiveness, which will become increasingly important as quality measures evolve and become more relevant to consumer decision making. However, although it is frequently assumed, the link between purchasing cooperatives and reduced administrative costs is less clear. Since each small employer must receive a bill and submit a premium payment for processing, the source of presumed administrative savings in comparison with small firms purchasing independently is not obvious. In the absence of empirical data to support the assumption that purchasing cooperatives reduce administrative costs, this analysis does not assume reduced administrative costs.

Evaluating the responsiveness of the purchasing cooperative to differentiation costs requires specification of the rating structure to be used inside the cooperative. As in the market outside the cooperative, the level of differentiation costs inside the cooperative is linked to the rating structure: the more restrictive the rating, the lower the differentiation costs. Incentive for the exit of low-risk small firms from the cooperative depends on the degree to which the cooperative's internal rules match the market rules outside the cooperative. A close match between the internal rules of the pool and the rating structure outside the pool is critical to preventing debilitating adverse selection against the cooperative. Consider the consequences of widely divergent rating systems (assuming guaranteed issue). If the pool features pure community rating and the market features unrestricted risk rating, the old and the sick will obtain a better deal inside the pool than they can outside. The young and healthy will exit the pool to obtain rates adjusted for age and health status outside the pool. The predicted result is eventual weakening, and possibly collapse, of the cooperative. Thus, if the market outside the pool has unrestricted rating and medical underwriting, the pool should as well. The same problems arise when market rules exist but are substantially more flexible than the internal pool rating structure. To eliminate differential attraction to the cooperative of relatively high-risk enrollees, the rating structures outside and inside the purchasing cooperative should match.

Purchasing cooperatives can be an effective response to the disadvantages of small firms with respect to both differentiation costs and scale issues. However, a cooperative that is unsupported by closely matching market rules will be unlikely to succeed.

Comparative Assessment of Market Structures

A comparative assessment of the structures considered in response to the difficulties encountered by small firms in the health insurance market is presented in Table 1.4. Each alternative is assessed individually, and the findings are summarized in the table. The key question is the responsiveness of the structure to the issues of concern, which are identified as threefold: risk

**TABLE 1.4 Responsiveness of Governance Structures
to Health Insurance Transaction Features**

	Small Firm, No Rules^	Lump Sum Transfers^^	Market Rules*	Purchasing Cooperative, No Rules**	Purchasing Cooperative, Market Rules***
Risk Differentiation	—	—	++	++	++
Economies of Scale	—	—	—	++	++
Low-Risk Exit Incentive	++	++	?	—	++

Legend: ++ Responsive   — Unresponsive   ? Inconclusive

Notes: ^ Absence of rules implies full risk rating.
^^ Cochrane's (1995) contractual approach using transfers between account and insurer.
* Assumes community rating by class, along with guaranteed issue and renewal; individual market remains fully risk rated.
** Assumes community rating by class, guaranteed issue, and guaranteed renewal inside the cooperative but no market rules outside the cooperative.
*** Assumes community rating by class, guaranteed issue, and guaranteed renewal both inside and outside the cooperative.

differentiation costs, economies of scale, and the incentive for low-risk employees to exit. If a mode of organization is relatively effective at managing an issue, it is rated as responsive and receives a "++" in the table. Less effective structures are considered unresponsive and are assigned a " — " score in the table.

Small Firm, No Rules

The small firm purchasing insurance on the market without rules is presumably assessed using full risk rating, including underwriting at the level of the individual employee for the smallest firms. Due to the high costs associated with full risk rating, this governance structure scores badly on risk differentiation costs, but does well on low-risk incentive to exit because full risk rating incorporates no cross-subsidy. Economies of scale are lacking in this mode.

- Risk Differentiation Costs: Unresponsive
- Economies of Scale: Unresponsive
- Low-Risk Exit Incentive: Responsive

Lump Sum Transfers

Lump sum transfers between a consumer's health insurance account and his or her insurer, the contractual solution to lifetime risk variability proposed by Cochrane (1995), looks much like the small firm in terms of responsiveness but is saddled with significant additional transaction costs. Again, full risk rating is assumed, resulting in high differentiation costs but little incentive for the low risks to exit.

- Risk Differentiation Costs: Unresponsive
- Economies of Scale: Unresponsive
- Low-Risk Exit Incentive: Responsive

Market Rules

Market rules reduce differentiation costs by restricting rates and ameliorating incentives for underwriting; here, community rating by class is the assumed rating mechanism. Whether shifting from full risk rating to community rating by class motivates low-risk firms to exit the small group market in favor of the fully risk-rated individual market is not clear. Community rating by class would raise rates somewhat for the lowest risk firms, but would have a much smaller impact on premiums than would pure community rating (American Academy of Actuaries 1993). Market rules do not address scale issues faced by small firms in terms of administrative costs, expertise, or choice.

- Risk Differentiation Costs: Responsive
- Economies of Scale: Unresponsive
- Low-Risk Exit Incentive: Inconclusive

Purchasing Cooperative, No Rules

Purchasing cooperatives address economies of scale in the areas of purchasing expertise and choice of health plan by bringing together a large number of small firms to form a collective. Assuming that the cooperative adopts some form of restricted rating internally, this mode also reduces risk differentiation costs. However, purchasing cooperatives that are unsupported by market rules will be vulnerable to low-risk exit from the cooperative to the outside market. To reduce risk differentiation costs, a cooperative must adopt a rating scheme that compresses premium variation and ameliorates the advantages of underwriting, such as community rating by class. But if the outside market retains full risk rating, low-risk small firms will exit the cooperative in favor of market discounts.

- Risk Differentiation Costs: Responsive
- Economies of Scale: Responsive
- Low-Risk Exit Incentive: Unresponsive

Purchasing Cooperative, Market Rules

Purchasing cooperatives supported by market rules appear to have a comparative advantage in managing the health insurance transaction of the small firm. If a community rating by class scheme prevails both inside the cooperative and in the outside market, risk differentiation costs can be reduced for the entire market. Further, the purchasing cooperative provides economies of scale — again, in relation to purchasing sophistication and choice of plan — for small firms that are unavailable in the outside market. As long as the individual market remains fully risk-rated, there will be some incentive for low-risk small employers to drop coverage and purchase individual policies. But identical rating rules in the small group market both inside and outside the purchasing cooperative ensures that low-risk small firms will not exit the cooperative to access market discounts.

- Risk Differentiation Costs: Responsive
- Economies of Scale: Responsive
- Low-Risk Exit Incentive: Responsive

The comparison indicates that two of the issues — risk differentiation and the incentive for low-risks to exit the market — revolve around the restrictiveness of the rating scheme, with a clear trade-off: more restrictive rating lowers differentiation costs but increases the incentive for low-risk employees to exit the market. Achieving economies of scale, by contrast, depends upon whether small firms join together to access the advantages experienced by large-firm purchasers; of the alternatives considered here, purchasing cooperatives are the only structure responsive to this concern.

Refutable Implications

The foregoing comparative analyses — both of small firms and large firms, and of alternative approaches to reorganizing the market for small firms — yield a number of refutable implications, each of which will be addressed in turn.

- Market rules will emerge in the market for small firms but not in the market for large firms.
- Where they arise, market rules on rating restrictions will take the form of community rating by class rather than pure community rating.
- Purchasing cooperatives will emerge in the market for small firms but not in the market for large firms.
- Purchasing cooperatives in the small-firm market will arise only where market rules exist to support them, and their internal rating structures will match the market rules.
- Where purchasing cooperatives supported by matching market rules exist, they will be the preferred form of market structure for small firms purchasing health care coverage.

Emergence of Market Rules, by Firm Size

Is it the case that market rules have arisen in the market for small firms but not in the market for large firms? The answer is clearly affirmative. A total of 45 states passed laws setting new rules in the market for small firms purchasing health insurance between 1990 and 1994 (General Accounting Office 1995). By contrast, no state issued regulations in the market for large firms. The argument could be made that this is in part because states have little real regulatory authority over the employee benefit activities of large firms due to ERISA. However, Congress, which does have the authority to regulate the employee benefit activities of large firms, also focused on small firms with its

Health Insurance Portability and Accountability Act of 1996. Although the law establishes portability requirements[16] for both small and large firms, it guarantees issue and renewal of products only for small groups, defined as firms with 2–50 employees.[17]

Dominance of Community Rating by Class

Is it the case, as we would expect based on this analysis, that adopted market rules feature community rating by class rather than pure community rating? Community rating by class achieves much of the reduction in differentiation costs with a much smaller redistribution component and less incentive for low-risk exit than pure community rating entails. A review of the market rules restricting rates in the small group market that were passed by 45 states during the early 1990s reveals that only one state — New York — adopted pure community rating (Chollet and Paul 1994; General Accounting Office 1995). The other states adopted either community rating by class or a more complex version of rating allowing for somewhat more detailed risk classification.

Emergence of Purchasing Cooperatives by Firm Size

While the regulatory activity seems consistent with the analytic distinction developed here between large and small firms, purchasing cooperative emergence is less clear-cut. Rather than the expected proliferation of purchasing cooperatives for small firms and absence of such mechanisms for large firms, cooperatives have arisen in some small-firm markets but not others, and have emerged in many large-firm markets. Two questions result. First, why haven't more purchasing cooperatives for small firms appeared, given their advantages in governing the health insurance transaction for small firms? Second, given that large firms presumably already enjoy the features that purchasing cooperatives bring to management of the health insurance transaction, why have purchasing cooperatives for large firms emerged?

Consider the first question first: why have cooperatives appeared in some small-firm markets but not others? The establishment of a purchasing cooperative for small firms requires the investment of start-up time and capital, and collective action on the part of small businesses may present an obstacle. In some cases, collective action problems have been overcome by state intervention; a number of states have passed legislation creating purchasing cooperatives for small firms. Other states, rather than becoming involved in private-sector structures, have passed legislation encouraging the creation of — and setting guidelines for — small-employer cooperatives (Alpha Center 1996). Numerous measures that would establish or regulate purchasing alliances for small firms have been considered at the federal level, but none of them have progressed very far. This is a question that merits further investigation.

Turn now to the query regarding the emergence of large-firm purchasing cooperatives. One response is that while small-firm cooperatives virtually always focus on collectively purchasing health insurance, many large-firm cooperatives do not actually purchase. Rather, they collaborate. Large firms have frequently joined forces for such activities as satisfaction surveys of employees, quality improvement initiatives, collection and analysis of utilization data, and standardization of benefit packages to enhance price and quality comparability across plans. These activities all entail significant cost, and sharing them across firms reduces the cost and makes carrying them out more feasible. Other large firms do create alliances that actually negotiate with health plans and purchase coverage for their employees. The reason that some large firms participate in purchasing cooperatives is worth investigating.

Cooperatives Supported by Matching Market Rules

When low-risk small employers are able to obtain risk-adjusted premiums outside the cooperative but not inside the cooperative, they will have an incentive to forego joining or to exit the cooperative. Thus, we would expect that cooperatives will emerge only where market rules exist, and that cooperatives will adopt the rating structure of the outside market.

Reference to existing cooperatives and market rules is instructive in this case. The key issue appears to be not the existence of market rules but rather a match between the rating practices of the cooperative and the rating structure in the outside market. Purchasing cooperatives may still arise if the market is fully risk rated, but in this case the cooperative must also be risk rated;

otherwise, the cooperative will bleed its low risks to the outside market, or will attract higher-than-average risks unable to obtain coverage as affordable elsewhere.

Exactly this phenomenon began to occur at the oldest private purchasing pool for small employers, the Council of Smaller Employers (COSE) in Cleveland. The nonprofit cooperative began operating in 1973 and now covers 200,000 enrollees who join through the Cleveland Chamber of Commerce. In Ohio's unreformed market, COSE was unable to succeed without mirroring the underwriting practices outside the cooperative. "Although COSE originally required its carriers to accept all applicants, it decided to allow underwriting in 1983 because it had attracted many older and sicker individuals who could not obtain coverage elsewhere. By screening for and denying coverage to people who are sick or at risk, Blue Cross can lower its costs and thus offer lower rates to COSE members" (General Accounting Office 1994 p. 29). Other cooperatives attempting to implement a more restrictive rating structure inside the cooperative than outside the cooperative, such as the Texas Insurance Purchasing Alliance (TIPA), have experienced similar problems. The TIPA has been called the "'poster child' for what happens in 'the not-fully-reformed state'" (*State Health Watch* 1996 p. 8).

Note that a cooperative that mirrors market risk-rating to ensure survival retains economies-of-scale advantages over small firms purchasing health insurance individually, but is unable to reduce differentiation costs relative to the outside market for small firms.

Dominance of Purchasing Cooperatives Supported by Market Rules

This analysis indicates that purchasing cooperatives that are supported by matching rating restrictions in the outside market provide a governance structure for small firms purchasing health insurance that has advantages over market rules alone or purchasing cooperatives without market rules. The implication is that where purchasing cooperatives supported by market rules exist, they will be the preferred mode of acquiring health care coverage. To investigate this prediction, the next section looks at California, where 1992 reforms resulted in the creation of both market rules and a purchasing cooperative.

The Case of California

Aggregate figures, such as the number of states that have passed legislation regulating the small-firm market for health insurance, can be very useful in assessing whether analytic predictions are borne out, at least in part, by existing structures. However, a detailed look at a single case can provide information that summary statistics cannot provide. This section presents an in-depth assessment of California's market for small-firm health insurance, comparing the structures that have emerged to the preceding analytic predictions, including the prediction that purchasing cooperatives supported by matching market rules will dominate other modes of purchasing insurance for small firms.

In 1992, California passed Assembly Bill 1672, establishing a set of market rules for insurers of small firms (3–50 employees) and creating a publicly run purchasing cooperative for private small employers, the Health Insurance Plan of California (HIPC) (California Statutes 1992).[18] The market rules include guaranteed issue, guaranteed renewal, limits on pre-existing condition exclusions, and rating restrictions. The rating scheme is community rating by class, and rating factors are limited to geographic area, family status, and age; sex is not allowed as a class adjustment.[19] An additional feature, called a rate band, allows insurers a small degree of flexibility in adjusting rates for other factors believed to contribute to health risk. The rate band allows insurers to charge the highest-risk firms a 10 percent surcharge, and to give the lowest-risk firms a 10 percent discount.[20] The rules also restrict the amount that insurers are allowed to raise or lower premiums from one year to the next.[21]

California's purchasing cooperative, The Health Insurance Plan of California (HIPC), functions as an intermediary between small employers and health plans, collecting premiums from small employers and distributing them to health plans. The Managed Risk Medical Insurance Board (MRMIB), a state agency within the Department of Health, is responsible for the HIPC. The Board and its staff handle policy decisions and negotiations and contracting with participating health plans; daily operations are contracted out to Employers Health Insurance, which handles enrollment, marketing, and data collection. The HIPC had enrolled approximately 124,000 employees and dependents as of April 1997.

The HIPC offers a wide selection of managed care plans, and the employees of small employers who join the HIPC may choose from any health plan the HIPC offers in their geographic region. During the 1996–97 enrollment year, the HIPC offered a total of 21 Health Maintenance Organizations (HMO),[22] three Preferred Provider Organizations (PPO), and three Point-of-Service (POS) plans in some or all parts of the state.[23]

The small group market regulations apply both inside and outside the HIPC, with one exception: the HIPC does not use rate bands. Inside the HIPC, premiums vary solely due to geographic region, family structure, and age. The absence of rate bands eliminates even limited adjustment for claims history or health status.

A summary of the attributes of the market rules and the HIPC with respect to the health insurance transaction are presented in Table 1.5, with small-firm and large-firm attributes reiterated for comparison. Small firms are disadvantaged in all respects in comparison with large firms. California's market rules address issues pertaining to risk differentiation but not to economies of scale; the HIPC addresses both sets of issues, at least partially.

The foregoing analysis of small group market structures, the specific features of California's market rules and the HIPC, and the comparative presentation in Table 1.5 raise several questions regarding California's reforms. First, what have been the effects of different rating structures inside and outside the HIPC? The HIPC is supported by market rules that regulate premiums, but the rates inside the HIPC are more restrictive than outside the

TABLE 1.5 Attributes of Governance Structures

	Small Firm	Large Firm	Market Rules	HIPC
Risk Differentiation				
Underwriting	—	++	++	++
Screening at Renewal	—	++	++	++
Economies of Scale				
Administrative Costs	—	++	—	??
Expertise	—	++	—	++
Choice	—	++	—	++

Legend: ++ Low Cost / Adequate   ?? Inconclusive   — Costly / Inadequate

HIPC, where insurers can use the rate bands. Has the HIPC attracted a riskier-than-average population? Second, given that the individual market has remained fully risk rated, have significant numbers of low-risk small employers left the small group market? The new rules — particularly guaranteed issue in conjunction with rating restrictions — favor high-risk small firms. We would expect those high-risk firms previously denied coverage or offered coverage only at prohibitive rates to enter the market, raising rates for all and encouraging exit for low-risk firms. Third, given the apparent advantages of the HIPC, why hasn't every small employer joined? One reason might be that the HIPC has attracted a riskier-than-average population due to its rating structure; is this the case? If not, what are the reasons? Each of these questions is addressed below.

The HIPC: Has Absence of Rate Bands Attracted High-Risk Small Firms?

The use of rate bands in the outside market but not in the HIPC raises the possibility that the HIPC will attract a disproportionate number of high-risk small employers who can obtain health care coverage without a risk-related surcharge inside the HIPC. However, the HIPC does not appear to have suffered from such adverse selection (Buchmueller 1996b). A number of factors are likely contributing to the HIPC's sustainability. First, although the HIPC does feature a greater degree of cross-subsidy than does the outside market, the difference is not large. If we assume that plans that participate in the HIPC charge a similar rate for the same benefit package both inside and outside the purchasing cooperative, then the most a high-risk firm could save by entering the HIPC would be 10 percent — the maximum surcharge over its standard risk rate. Some firms will find this worthwhile, and we will expect the HIPC to enroll a larger proportion of high-risk firms than are found in the outside market.

However, assuming it does enroll a slightly riskier subscriber group than is representative of the market as a whole, the HIPC has several sources of potential savings that should help hold premiums down in spite of higher costs. The HIPC essentially eliminates differentiation costs by removing any incentive for risk assessment at the individual-employee level. Another source of savings is the purchasing power that more than 100,000 enrollees bring to the negotiating table. In addition, the HIPC provides a relatively inexpensive source of "lives" for participating health plans. Health plans can spend significant resources in acquiring new enrollees, either through advertising or through merger with or acquisition of other health plans. Joining the HIPC provides low-cost access to a large group of potential enrollees, saving acquisition costs that can be passed on to enrollees as lower premiums.

Low-Risk Exit from the Market Has Not Materialized

It was expected that increased cross-subsidization would result in higher rates for low-risk small firms. Some exit of low-risk subscribers was anticipated as a result but has not appeared to materialize. In fact, health insurance provision among the smallest firms (fewer than 10 employees) increased by 10–13 percent (Buchmueller and Jensen 1996). One contributing factor might be a competitive market that held premiums down for all firms. Buchmueller and Jensen (1996) found that after years of increasing premiums prior to 1993, premiums were flat or falling during the 1993–1995 period. It seems likely that the competitive rates may have stemmed the potential exodus of low-risk groups by reducing or eliminating their rate increases.

Another contributing factor might have been increased penetration of managed care into the small group market. Historically, small firms have offered a single health insurance plan, almost always fee-for-service. When only a single plan can be offered, fee-for-service plans make sense because each employee is assured access to his or her provider of choice. Furthermore, many HMOs have avoided small firms. HMOs tend to have less underwriting expertise than do commercial insurers; the widespread and aggressive underwriting practices of the commercial insurers made them formidable competitors, particularly considering the high degree of risk variability among small firms. Further, federally qualified HMOs must abide by restrictions on rating and underwriting practices.[24]

The dynamics of the market, however, have recently changed. Table 1.6 shows the shifting distribution of small-firm enrollment in various types of plans for the U.S. as a whole. Although a definitive connection cannot be drawn, it seems suggestive that between 1990 and 1994, 45 states created new rules for the small group market (General Accounting Office 1995). In California, the new market rules have leveled the playing field, reducing the

**TABLE 1.6   Percentage of Insured Workers,
By Plan Type and Firm Size, 1993 and 1995**

	1–24 Employees	25–49 Employees	All Firms
1993			
Conventional	78.3	65 .2	48.9
HMO	8.2	10.9	22.4
PPO	9.9	11.8	19.6
Point-of-service	3.6	12.1	9.1
1995			
Conventional	30.5	30.2	27.4
HMO	19.2	38.9	27.5
PPO	26.8	21.4	25.0
Point-of-service	23.5	9.5	20.1

Source: Jensen et al. (1997). Data from KPMG Peat Marwick/Wayne State University survey.

importance of underwriting expertise. Managed care organizations appear to have responded by increasing their participation in the small group market.

A competitive market and increased managed care penetration may have reduced the exit of low-risk small firms from the market, but it is not clear that any mass exodus would have occurred in lieu of these factors. The rating rules, while restrictive in comparison with the pre-1992 market, allow premiums to incorporate a significant degree of risk variation, particularly since age is included as a class. A simulation by the American Academy of Actuaries found that while 30 percent of small-firm employees would experience a rate increase of at least 20 percent in a switch from unrestricted rating to pure community rating, only 9 percent were expected to receive a similar rate increase under community rating with class adjustments (American Academy of Actuaries 1993).

The HIPC: Why Not All Small Firms?

The HIPC appears to dominate the market rules in the advantages it brings to the health insurance transaction. In addition to reducing risk differentiation costs, it provides a wide choice of health plans at the employee level, and shifts the burden of deciphering the complex health insurance market from the employer to the purchasing cooperative. The cooperative, rather than the employer, must evaluate the plans to ensure that their delivery networks and medical care quality are adequate. Given the obvious advantages, why hasn't every small firm in the state flocked to join the HIPC? Although 124,000 enrollees as of March 1997 certainly represents a significant and respectable enrollment, it represents only a tiny fraction of the estimated 4–8 million employees and dependents in the small group market. In responding to this question, it is important to differentiate between two groups of small firms that have chosen not to join the HIPC: those that offer health care coverage and those that do not. Consider each in turn.

The HIPC offers a specific type of health care coverage that appeals to some firms but not to others. The HIPC provides choice, but it is primarily choice among HMOs with a standard benefit package. Firms interested in other products and other benefit designs will not be attracted to the HIPC. Some firms will prefer to retain their fee-for-service policies, rather than convert to the HIPC's managed care plans. Other firms already offer managed care but in the form of PPOs, of which the HIPC offers only a few. Further, although the standard benefit package may appeal to employers due to enhanced ability to compare prices across plans, some employers will want a different benefit package than is offered through the HIPC. In some cases, the HIPC benefit package is more generous than the firm is able to afford or wants to purchase; a thinner benefit package, such as one that features high copayments or a large deductible, can be purchased from an insurer outside the HIPC. The HIPC's strongest appeal will be among small firms that want to enroll in HMOs and whose needs are met by the provisions of the standard benefit package.

Although the HIPC includes most of the health plans that sell health care coverage in the small group market, a few insurers that have a large share of the small group market have declined to join the HIPC, most notably Blue Cross of California. Blue Cross has developed an internal choice model, with "dual choice" products that allow some employees from a firm to join an HMO while others join a PPO. Firms whose employees are satisfied with Blue Cross coverage will see little reason to switch.

A 1995 survey, performed two years after the implementation of the HIPC, found that many small employers were unaware of the HIPC's existence (Buchmueller 1996a). Of those employers who knew of the HIPC but continued to offer other insurance, the most important reason was satisfaction with current coverage. Other factors mentioned included that the firm could obtain lower premiums outside the HIPC, that the firm's agent had advised against joining the HIPC, and that the firm's current insurer was not available inside the HIPC.

Lack of awareness of the HIPC may be one reason that firms that do not offer health care coverage decline to join the HIPC, but cost is likely to be at least as important. Although this question has not been studied specifically with respect to California small firms and the HIPC, numerous national surveys of small employers have found that cost is the key reason for not providing coverage (Hall and Kuder 1990; Health Insurance Association of America 1990; Helms et al. 1992; Morrisey et al. 1994). However, even when the cost of coverage is lowered substantially, only a small number of firms purchase coverage (Helms et al. 1992; McLaughlin and Zellers 1992). In spite of the reluctance of many small firms to offer coverage, the HIPC appears to have had some effect in encouraging firms that had not previously offered coverage to begin to do so; approximately 20 percent of the HIPC's enrollees work for firms that had not offered health benefits prior to joining the HIPC. The number of these firms that would have purchased coverage regardless of the existence of the HIPC is unknown.

Conclusion

The ability of firms to effectively purchase health insurance for their employees varies with firm size. Since small firms are unable to offer insurers predictable risk, high differentiation costs result in underwriting at the level of the individual employee. Small firms are further disadvantaged by relatively high administrative costs, lack of sophistication in the complex market for health care coverage, and narrow or no choice among coverage options. Given that employment-based access to health care coverage is solidly ensconced in the U.S., improving the small firm's ability to act as a health care purchaser merits consideration.

This analysis explores two mechanisms for improving the small firm as a governance structure for the health insurance transaction. One option, regulation of health insurers providing coverage to small firms, addresses risk variability issues and resulting differentiation costs, but does not deal with scale issues. A second option, purchasing cooperatives, addresses both risk variability and scale issues. However, an important caveat to the purchasing cooperative is the match between rating systems inside and outside the purchasing cooperative; without matching rating systems, the cooperative will likely attract an unfavorable risk profile and may eventually collapse. A second caveat is that, although the advantages of the cooperative as an intermediary for such issues as purchasing sophistication and choice of plan is clear, the presumed savings through premium and administrative cost reductions have yet to be closely examined empirically.

Prevalent structures for the purchase of health insurance by small firms generally bear out, at least in part, the implications of this analysis regarding the differential ability of small and large firms to effectively manage the health insurance transaction. The small firm behaves more like a consumer purchasing a retail good, while the large firm purchases health care coverage much as it would purchase other intermediate products. Not surprisingly, market rules have arisen to support small firms, but not large firms, in their attempt to purchase coverage. The pattern of emergence of purchasing cooperatives, however, raises a number of interesting questions. Why have they appeared in some small-firm markets but not others? Why do some large firms use cooperatives for purchasing, while others join collectives to collaborate on quality and employee satisfaction initiatives, and still others eschew cooperatives altogether? Perhaps most interesting, why don't more small employers take advantage of the apparent advantages provided by purchasing cooperatives? In one state that has adopted a purchasing cooperative supported by a near-matching rating structure in the outside market, the cooperative has had moderate success but has not borne out predictions regarding its dominance as a structure for small-firm health insurance purchasing. A logic of purchasing cooperatives that would explain their differential emergence and attraction for employers and employees of various sizes is needed.

APPENDIX:
Risk Variability and Firm Size

The law of large numbers, which is frequently cited as the statistical mechanism underlying insurance, can be summarized as follows: "Under this law, the impossibility of predicting a happening in an individual case is replaced by the demonstrable ability to forecast collective losses from a large number of cases" (Mehr 1986 p. 39). This can be stated more precisely by referring to the familiar statistical measures of central tendency and dispersion, the mean and variance. The true mean and variance of a statistical population are always unknown, unless each element of the population can be measured and exact values calculated, but sampling theory provides a basis for describing the unknown population values using known sample data.

Eq. 1: Population Mean

$$\mu = E(x)$$

Eq. 2: Population Variance

$$\sigma^2 = E(x - E(x))^2$$

Eq. 3: Sample Mean

$$\bar{x} = \frac{\sum x}{n}$$

Eq. 4: Sample Variance

$$s^2 = \frac{\sum (x - \bar{x})^2}{n - 1}$$

Eq. 5: Sample Standard Deviation

$$s = \sqrt{\frac{\sum (x - \bar{x})^2}{n - 1}}$$

The mean and variance of the sample are interesting to insurers, but the mean and variance of the distribution of the sample mean are of particular interest because insurers are most interested in the accuracy of their estimates of average losses. As long as the healthy members of a group balance out the sick members, on average, insurers need not concern themselves with the loss values associated with individual members of the group. The mean and variance of the distribution of the sample mean can be usefully conceptualized in a repeated sampling context. That is, if one takes a number of samples of size *n* from a population, then each of those samples will have a mean, and those sample means will have a mean and a variance of their own, separate from the mean and the variance of any one sample. It can be shown mathematically that the expected value of the distribution of the sample mean will be equal to the population mean and that the variance of the distribution of the sample mean will be inversely proportional to the size of the sample (Armitage and Berry 1987 p. 84; Ramanathan 1993 p. 129).

Eq. 6: Mean of the Distribution of the Sample Mean $\qquad \mu_{\bar{x}} = \mu$

Eq. 7: Variance of the Distribution of the Sample Mean $\qquad \sigma_{\bar{x}}^2 = \dfrac{\sigma^2}{n}$

Eq. 8: Standard Error of the Mean $\qquad \sigma_{\bar{x}} = \sqrt{\dfrac{\sigma^2}{n}}$

The variance of the distribution of the sample mean is estimated by substituting the sample variance (s^2 in Eq. 4) for the population variance, σ^2 and dividing by the sample size, n Equation 7 provides a measure of the accuracy of the insurers' estimates, and it clearly demonstrates how the accuracy of the estimate increases (the variance shrinks) as sample size increases. The standard deviation of the distribution of the sample mean is given by the square root of the variance of the distribution of the sample mean (Eq. 8). This term is often called the standard error of the mean.

An example will demonstrate the relationship between group size and prediction accuracy. Consider two firms, one with ten employees and one with 1000. In deciding what premium to charge these groups, an insurer examines medical expenditures from the prior year. The values for the ten employees are as follows (in dollars): 0, 100, 300, 600, 900, 1000, 1200, 1500, 1800, and 2000. The values for the 1000 employees have an identical distribution, with each value observed 100 times (*i.e.*, 100 employees had no medical expenditures in the previous year, 100 employees incurred $100 in medical expenditures, and so forth). For each firm, the average value of medical expenditures in the previous year is $940, given by Equation 3. Equations 4 and 5 yield the sample variance and standard deviation for each firm. The ten-employee firm has a variance of 484,889 and a standard deviation of 696. The 1000-employee firm has a similar variance and standard deviation: 436,837 and 661. However, the variance of the distribution of the sample mean and its square root, the standard error, are quite different. For the ten-employee firm, the variance of the distribution of the sample mean is 48,488.9 and the standard error is 220.2, while the values for the 1000-employee firm are 436.8 and 20.9.

The meaning of these differences is demonstrated in Table 1.7. The standard error gives an estimate of the precision of the sample mean. If we assume that the expenditures for the current year will follow the same

TABLE 1.7   Accuracy of Estimated Sample Mean

N	Mean	Std Error	68.26% (1 std deviation)		95.44% (2 std deviations)		99.74% (3 std deviations)	
			Low	High	Low	High	Low	High
10	940	220.2	719.8	1160.2	499.6	1380.4	279.4	1600.6
1000	940	20.9	919.1	960.9	898.2	981.8	877.3	1002.7

pattern as the previous year's expenditures, then we can assert with 68 percent certainty that the average expenditure in the 1000-employee firm will fall between $919.10 and $960.90. By contrast, we can say with the same degree of certainty about the ten-employee group only that average expenditures will fall between $719.80 and $1,160.20. The gap widens as we increase our demands for accuracy to 95 percent certainty and to almost 100 percent certainty.

Notes

1   For an introduction to transaction cost economics, see Williamson (1979; 1991; 1994).

2   The governance structure is the institutional mode in which the transaction is organized. Williamson (1975; 1985) examines the trade-offs between organizing transactions inside the firm ("make") and outside the firm ("buy"), and develops the characteristics of two of the most familiar governance structures: the firm and the marketplace.

3   A mechanism is an instrument for modifying the ability of a governance structure to manage a transaction. Two broad categories of mechanisms are contracting and regulatory activities. Mechanisms may create new governance structures, as is the case with purchasing cooperatives.

4   The reduced wage more closely estimates their true productivity level, but it is perceived as a loss relative to the average wage level. The transfer reduces the level of cross-subsidization from the more to the less productive workers.

5   In 1993, of 226.2 million people under 65 in the U.S., 61 percent were insured through employers, 16 percent through public programs, 9 percent through private individual policies, and 18 percent were uninsured. Numbers do not add up to 100 because individuals may have more than one type of coverage (Silverman et al., 1995, Table 8.1).

6   According to 1993 survey data, 4 percent of employers offer flexible benefit plans (Silverman et al., 1995, Table 15.5, p. 556).

7   The survey polled three separate groups: commercial insurers, Blue Cross/Blue Shield plans, and Health Maintenance Organizations. The results reported here refer to the commercial insurer responses.

8   Note that an employee who is insured elsewhere, such as through a spouse's place of employment, is considered to have "waived" rather than "declined" coverage. If that source of coverage is lost, the employee can generally join his or her own employer-sponsored

coverage without providing evidence of insurability for a specified period of time, often 30 days.

9   For a detailed explanation of self-insurance, the distinction between self-insurance and self-funding, and the difference between partially and fully self-insuring, see McDonnell, et al. (1986).

10   In addition to adding to the cost of coverage, state-mandated benefits can be particularly problematic for firms that operate across state lines — generally larger firms — since each state may mandate a different package of benefits.

11   Large firms purchase either insurance coverage or medical care as an intermediate product, depending on whether they are fully insured or self-insured.

12   Whether all products sold by the insurer must be offered to all small firms, or whether insurers are allowed to sell just one or two specialized products to firms that would not otherwise qualify for health care coverage, is a policy issue that varies from state to state.

13   For example, many policies include a minimum participation requirement: At least a specified percentage, such as 70 percent, of the employees in the firm who are eligible for the insurance must purchase it. This provision is intended to protect the insurer from the adverse selection that would result if only the highest-risk employees signed on.

14   A vigorous debate has arisen over redistribution through community rating in the health insurance market, pitting efficiency advocates with adherents of social justice. See, for example, Stone (1993) and Daniels (1990) for the argument in favor of cross-subsidization, and Clifford and Iuculano (1987) and Epstein (1996) for the argument against. Hall (1994) provides a balanced view of both sides of the issue.

15   Regulation of MEWAs is a complex area. Responding to MEWA claims that they were exempt from state regulation under the Employee Retirement Income Security Act (ERISA), the federal government passed clarifying legislation in 1983 to establish state jurisdiction over MEWAs that are run by insurance companies rather than by employers. However, confusion continues. Often, states do not realize that MEWAs even exist until they go bankrupt, leaving behind unpaid medical bills and uninsured participants (General Accounting Office 1992).

16   Portability refers to the ability of the employee to transfer health care coverage from an old job to a new job without the renewed imposition of pre-existing condition exclusions. Generally, portability provisions require that insurers accept "time served" with a prior insurer for pre-existing conditions as credit toward the allowable exclusion period. Thus, if insurers are allowed to exclude pre-existing conditions for 12 months, an employee with six months of coverage at one job will have no more than six more months of exclusion under a new job's insurer.

17   The absence of rate restrictions in the law's provisions means that the law's small-group market measures have little real impact; all an insurer need do to avoid selling coverage to a group is to set the premiums so high that the coverage becomes unattractive. However, the law specifies that it is not intended to pre-empt more far-reaching state-level measures, so it will not reverse state-level reforms that go beyond the federal law's provisions.

18   California's reforms were phased in over several years. During the first year, reforms applied to employers with between 5 and 50 employees; the minimum firm size decreased to 4 employees in July 1994 and 3 employees in July 1995. The minimum firm size was subsequently further decreased to 2 employees to bring California into compliance with the federal Health Insurance Portability and Accountability Act of 1996.

19   Insurers may include up to 9 geographic regions, 7 age groups, and 4 family structures in their rate tables for each benefit plan design. The age and family categories are defined in the law; insurers have more flexibility with geographic region. While the law provides some

restrictions — a region cannot be smaller than a county, which prevents border gerrymandering to segment the market by risk — insurers can set their own boundaries. Each insurer is required by law to develop a grid of "standard employee risk rates" for each of its health plan designs; the grid is composed of cells for each age/family status/geographic area combination used by the insurer. The standard rate is not an average rate but rather a rate that the insurer would charge for an individual representing an average risk.

20   Like the definition of firm size, the width of the rate band was phased in over several years. Initially, the rate band was set at plus or minus 20 percent of the standard rate. The width was halved to its final value of 10 percent in July 1996. If the rate band is 20 percent, the maximum rate can be no more than 1.5 times the minimum rate charged to an employer group with the same characteristics (geographic region, age, family structure, health plan). The 10 percent rate band reduces the multiple to 1.2.

21   Insurers are prohibited from raising premiums more than 10 percentage points relative to the standard rate in any given year. For example, an employer receiving 90 percent of the standard rate during the first year cannot receive a rate that is more than 100 percent of the standard rate during the second year, even though the maximum rate allowed by law is 110 percent of standard.

22   The HMO count includes one plan called an Exclusive Provider Organization, which from the consumer perspective is indistinguishable from an HMO.

23   Point-of-service is a hybrid of the comprehensive coverage of HMOs and freedom of provider choice in conventional plans; in-network care is generally provided with minimal cost-sharing, while out-of-network care offers freedom of choice but entails substantially more cost-sharing.

24   Federal qualification under the Health Maintenance Organization Act of 1973 is voluntary; in 1993, approximately 58 percent of HMOs were federally qualified, enrolling about 76 percent of all HMO enrollees (Group Health Association of America 1994). To obtain federal qualification, HMOs must offer a specified minimum benefit package, limit cost-sharing, and abide by restrictions on rating and underwriting. In the past, federal qualification has signaled quality to potential enrollees, but its value has declined as more direct (although still imperfect) methods of quality assessment, such as HEDIS (Health Plan and Employer Data Information Set), have been adopted.

References

Acs, G., Long, S. H., Marquis, M. S., and Short, P.F. (1996). "Self-Insured Employer Health Plans: Prevalence, Profile, Provisions, and Premiums." *Health Affairs*, 15(2), 266–278.

Alpha Center. (1996). "Technical Assistance Memorandum #9: Health Insurance Market Reforms and Pooled Purchasing: Select State Provisions."

American Academy of Actuaries. (1993). "An Analysis of Mandated Community Rating."

Armitage, P., and Berry, G. (1987). *Statistical Methods in Medical Research*. Blackwell Scientific Publications, Oxford.

Arrow, K.J. (1963). "Uncertainty and the Welfare Economics of Medical Care." *American Economic Review*, 53(5), 941–973.

Barzel, Y. (1977). "Some Fallacies in the Interpretation of Information Costs." *Journal of Law and Economics*, 20(2), 291–306.

Buchmueller, T.C. (1996a). "Government Sponsored Employer Purchasing Cooperatives: The Early Experience of the Health Insurance Plan of California." Manuscript.

Buchmueller, T.C. (1996b). "Managed Competition in the Small Group Health Insurance Market: The Early Experience of California's HIPC." Manuscript.

Buchmueller, T.C., and Jensen, G.A. (1996). "Small Group Reform in a Competitive Managed Care Market: The Case of California, 1993 to 1995." Manuscript.

California Statutes. (1992). "Chapter 1128."

Cantor, J.C., Long, S.H., and Marquis, M.S. (1995). "Private Employment-Based Health Insurance In Ten States." *Health Affairs*, 14(2), 198–209.

Chollet, D.J., and Paul, R.R. (1994). "Community Rating: Issues and Experiences." Alpha Center. Washington, D.C. December.

Clifford, K., and Iuculano, R. (1987). "AIDS and Insurance: The Rationale for AIDS-Related Testing." *Harvard Law Review*, 100, 1806–24.

Cochrane, J.H. (1995). "Time-Consistent Health Insurance." *Journal of Political Economy*, 103(3), 445–473.

Congressional Research Service. (1988). *Insuring the Uninsured: Options and Analysis*. U.S. Government Printing Office, Washington, D.C.

Congressional Research Service. (1990). *Private Health Insurance: Options for Reform*. U.S. Government Printing Office, Washington, D.C.

Daniels, N. (1990). "Insurability and the HIV Epidemic: Ethical Issues in Underwriting." *Milbank Quarterly*, 68(4), 497–525.

Dowd, B., and Feldman, R. (1992). "Insurer Competition and Protection from Risk Redefinition in the Individual and Small Group Health Insurance Market." *Inquiry*, 29, 148–157.

Eden, J., Mount, L., and Miike, L. (1988). *AIDS and Health Insurance: An OTA Survey*. Office of Technology Assessment; U.S. Government Printing Office, Washington, D.C.

Epstein, R. A. (1996). "Antidiscrimination in Health Care." The Independent Institute. Oakland, California.

General Accounting Office. (1992). "Employee Benefits: States Need Labor's Help Regulating Multiple Employer Welfare Arrangements." HRD–92–40. March.

General Accounting Office. (1994). "Access to Health Insurance: Public and Private Employers' Experience With Purchasing Cooperatives." HEHS–94–142. May.

General Accounting Office. (1995). "Health Insurance Regulation: Variation in Recent State Small Employer Health Insurance Reforms." HEHS–95–161FS.

Gregg, D.W. (1973). "Fundamental Characteristics of Group Insurance." *Life and Health Insurance Handbook*, D.W. Gregg and V.B. Lucas, eds., Richard D. Irwin, Inc., Homewood, Illinois, 351–371.

Group Health Association of America. (1994). *HMO Industry Profile*. GHAA, Washington, D.C.

Hall, C.P., Jr., and Kuder, J.M. (1990). *Small Business and Health Care: Results of a Survey*. The NFIB Foundation, Washington, D.C.

Hall, M.A. (1992). "Reforming the Health Insurance Market for Small Businesses." *New England Journal of Medicine*, 326(8), 565–570.

Hall, M.A. (1994). *Reforming Private Health Insurance*. AEI Press, Washington, D.C.

Health Insurance Association of America. (1990). "Providing Employee Health Benefits: How Firms Differ." Washington, D.C.

Helms, W.D., Gauthier, A.K., and Campion, D.M. (1992). "Mending The Flaws in the Small Group Market." *Health Affairs*, 11(2), 7–27.

Jensen, G.A., Morrisey, M.A., Gaffney, S., and Liston, D.K. (1997). "The New Dominance of Managed Care: Insurance Trends In The 1990s." *Health Affairs*, 16(1), 125–136.

Kenney, R.W., and Klein, B. (1983). "The Economics of Block Booking." *Journal of Law and Economics*, 26, 497–540.

Long, J.E. (1992). "Testimony of the National Association of Insurance Commissioners." *Multiple Employer Welfare Arrangements. Hearing Before the Subcommittee on Labor-Management Relations of the U.S. House of Representatives.*

Long, S.H., and Marquis, M. S. (1993). "Gaps in Employer Coverage: Lack of Supply or Lack of Demand?" *Health Affairs*, Supplement, 282–293.

McDonnell, P., Guttenberg, A., Greenberg, L., and Arnett, R.H., III. (1986). "Self-Insured Health Plans." *Health Care Financing Review*, 8(2), 1–16.

McLaughlin, C.G., and Zellers, W.K. (1992). "The Shortcomings of Voluntarism in the Small Group Insurance Market." *Health Affairs*, Summer, 28–40.

Mehr, R.I. (1986). *Fundamentals of Insurance*. Irwin, Homewood, Illinois.

Mehr, R.I., Cammack, E., and Rose, T. (1985). *Principles of Insurance*. Richard D. Irwin, Inc., Homewood, Illinois.

Morrisey, M.A., Jensen, G.A., and Morlock, R.A. (1994). "Small Employers and the Health Insurance Market." *Health Affairs*, 13(5), 149–161.

Pauly, M.V. (1970). "The Welfare Economics of Community Rating." *Journal of Risk and Insurance*, 37, 407–418.

Pauly, M.V. (1992). "Risk Variation and Fallback Insurers in Universal Coverage Insurance Plans." *Inquiry*, 29, 137–147.

Pupp, R.L. (1981). "Community Rating and Cross Subsidies in Health Insurance." *Journal of Risk and Insurance*, 48, 610–627.

Ramanathan, R. (1993). *Statistical Methods in Econometrics*. Academic Press, Inc., San Diego.

Schwartz, W. B. (1994). "In the Pipeline: A Wave of Valuable Medical Technology." *Health Affairs*, Summer, 70–79.

Silverman, C., Anzick, M., Boyce, S., Campbell, S., McDonnell, K., Reilly, A., and Snider, S. (1995). *EBRI Databook on Employee Benefits*, Employee Benefit Research Institute, Washington, D.C.

Spence, M. (1973). "Job Market Signaling." *Quarterly Journal of Economics*, 87, 355–374.

State Health Watch. (1996). "Private Purchasing Co-ops Show Rapid Growth in Several States." October.

Stone, D.A. (1993). "The Struggle for the Soul of Health Insurance." *Journal of Health Politics, Policy and Law*, 18(2), 287–317.

Sullivan, C.B., Miller, M., Feldman, R., and Dowd, B. (1992). "Employer-Sponsored Health Insurance in 1991." *Health Affairs*, 11(4), 172–185.

Thomas, G.W. (1973). "Group Underwriting and Reinsurance." *Life and Health Insurance Handbook*, D.W. Gregg and V.B. Lucas, eds., Richard D. Irwin, Inc., Homewood, Illinois, 433–449.

Trapnell, G. (1990). "Testimony by the Committee on Health, American Academy of Actuaries." *Health Insurance in the Small Group Market. Hearing Before the Subcommittee on Ways and Means, House of Representatives, 101st Congress*, U.S. Government Printing Office, Washington, D.C.

Tuller, D. (1989). "Health Coverage Ax to Hit Californians." *San Francisco Chronicle*. February 7. p. C1.

Williamson, O.E. (1975). *Markets and Hierarchies: Analysis and Antitrust Implications*. The Free Press, New York.

Williamson, O.E. (1979). "Transaction-Cost Economics: The Governance of Contractual Relations." *Journal of Law and Economics*, 22, 233–261.

Williamson, O.E. (1985). *The Economic Institutions of Capitalism*. The Free Press, New York.

Williamson, O.E. (1991). "Comparative Economic Organization: The Analysis of Discrete Structural Alternatives." *Administrative Science Quarterly*, 36, 269–296.

Williamson, O.E. (1994). "The Mechanisms of Governance: Prologue." Manuscript.

Williamson, O.E. (1995). "Hierarchies, Markets and Power in the Economy: An Economic Perspective." *Industrial and Corporate Change*, 4(1), 21–49.

Zellers, W. K., McLaughlin, C.G., and Frick, K.D. (1992). "Small-Business Health Insurance: Only the Healthy Need Apply." *Health Affairs*, Spring, 174–180.

2 The Political History of California's Reforms

Introduction[1]

In August 1992, the California state legislature passed a reform package setting strict new rules in the health insurance market for small employers and creating the first state-run purchasing cooperative for private small employers in the country. A 1993 Department of Insurance bulletin opined: "AB [Assembly Bill] 1672 may be the most dramatic single piece of health insurance regulation legislation yet enacted in California in terms of the fundamental changes it makes in the insurance market to which it applies" (California Department of Insurance 1993b).

The new market rules, applying to firms with between 5 and 50 employees and phasing down to a minimum of three employees over two years, guaranteed issue and renewal of health care coverage, restricted variability in premium levels among firms, and limited the use of pre-existing condition exclusions.[2] For the first time, every insurer providing health care coverage to even one small employer was required to offer coverage to any interested small employer. Further, the insurer was no longer allowed to sell certain plans to high-risk small employers and other plans to low-risk small employers; all plans now had to be available to all small firms. Insurers were no longer allowed to reject firms based on the risk level of their employees, or to charge more than 50 percent more (reduced to 22 percent after three years) for the highest-risk groups than they charged for the lowest-risk groups. Individual employees could no longer be excluded from group policies, and coverage could not be dropped in response to a period of high utilization. The legislation also created a voluntary alliance of small employers and assigned a state agency to serve as intermediary between the employers and health plans participating in the cooperative. The new purchasing cooperative was to provide extensive choice to the employees of small firms that joined and to allow small employers to access health care coverage at premiums generally available only to large firms.

Why did small group market reform pass in California in 1992? At first blush, it appeared destined to fail. The initiative seemed to pit the insurance industry against small employers in a battle between a powerful lobby for which the legislation was a central issue and a diverse and unorganized group of entrepreneurs for whom availability of health insurance was just one of many business concerns competing for attention. The changes to the status quo were fundamental, and they seemed to overwhelmingly benefit the small employers rather than the insurance industry. The successful passage and implementation of the reforms seem counterintuitive and demand an explanation.

This chapter argues that the climate surrounding the issue of access to health insurance was crucial to the passage of the reforms because it predisposed the insurance industry to consider small group reform as a way to head off more comprehensive insurance reform, including proposals that threatened their very existence. The argument is also made that, in addition to the support of the insurance industry, the other key factor in the passage of the reforms was the deep commitment of policymakers with diverse agendas to shepherding the changes through the legislative process.

Although the focus of this chapter is restricted to an in-depth study of a single policy, the conditions that allowed small group market reform to pass in California hold relevance for similar policy situations in other areas of the health field and in other fields. The obstacles to the passage of legislation in California — an organized group strongly affected by a prospective policy on one side of the legislation and an unorganized and diffusely affected group on the other — characterize an entire class of policy situations. The factors that came into play in California on the issue of small group market reform — interest group efforts to pre-empt more drastic change and the efforts of policy entrepreneurs on behalf of an unmobilized constituency — may prove important in a variety of applications to other issues both inside and outside California.

A second puzzle posed by the California reforms is their comprehensiveness. Compared to similar proposals in other states and to the model legislation created by the National Association for Insurance Commissioners, California's measures were extensive. If the insurance industry agreed to any reforms at all, token legislation to appease critics might have been expected instead of the far-reaching law that emerged. A key finding of the analysis that follows is that the fragmentation of the insurance industry prevented the unified front that might have resulted in a milder version of reform. The final outcome of the legislation went farther than any of the numerous industry coalitions proposed to go.

A final question relates to the sustainability of the reforms. Several years later, there is consensus that the reform package, judged within the constraints of its limited objectives, is a success. The rules have stabilized the health insurance market for small groups, ending the fluctuating premiums and abrupt cancellations that had plagued the market during the 1980s. The feared increases in premiums and resulting declines in employer-provided insurance have failed to materialize. The purchasing cooperative has enrolled more than 124,000 small employers, employees, and family members between July 1993 and March 1997, including 20 percent that previously were uninsured. Although this enrollment falls short of initial expectations (Russell 1993b) and represents a very small fraction of potential enrollment (Winterbottom et al. 1995), the cooperative provides an attractive option for thousands of Californians, offering a much wider selection of health plans than is generally available to employees of small firms.

That the reforms remain intact after more than four years cannot be taken for granted. What does California's post-passage implementation phase tell us about important conditions for the maintenance of a new status quo? Two key factors emerge. First, the continuing commitment of policymakers invested in maintaining the reforms. Second, a competitive health insurance market to help hold down the premium increases for some small firms that are the inevitable result of one of the central components of reform — redistribution.

Sparer (1994) has commented on a surprising lack of attention to state-level health care politics. Noting the importance of state financing of health care coverage and the role of state officials in Medicaid, regulation of the insurance sector, and in the provision of safety-net coverage, he points out that variation in state politics results in variation in state policies with regard to health care. This chapter attempts to illuminate the politics of health care in the state of California by tracing the evolution of perhaps the key piece of health insurance legislation to pass in a decade — small group market reform.

The next sections of the paper trace the evolution of small group market reform and its implementation in California. Initially, the main issue was expansion of coverage to the uninsured; Section 2 provides a brief overview of this debate. The discussion then shifted to the small group market; Section 3 characterizes the market, and describes the players, the issues, the proposals, and the outcome. Section 4 provides a brief account of the numerous proposals for comprehensive health care reform, all of which failed. In Sections 5 and 6, the paper discusses the implementation of the small group reforms and presents an overview of market-based purchasing alliances.

Section 7 presents a conceptual overview of the generic structural situation for which small group market reform provides a specific example. Section 8 then applies this framework to the case of small group market reform, in the process answering the question regarding the counterintuitive nature of the passage of the reforms. Section 9 addresses the relatively comprehensive nature of the reforms, and Section 10 discusses their sustainability. The final section comments on the current status of the reforms and the prospects for their expansion.

The Access Issue

At the national level, vigorous debate was underway in the late 1980s. The constantly cited number of 37 million uninsured Americans rang through the policy world. The number of uninsured had risen from 30.5 to 37.2 million between 1980 and 1986, from 13.7 to 15.7 percent of the population (Health Care Financing Administration 1996 p. 362, Table 73). Simultaneously, costs had risen drastically, almost doubling over the six-year period. Health care spending rose from $220.1 billion in 1980 to $414.5 billion in 1986, far outstripping growth in the gross domestic product (Health Care Financing Administration 1996 p. 188, Table 1). The U.S. Congress, private-sector interest groups, and academia all struggled for a solution.

In Congress, Senator Edward Kennedy and Representative Henry Waxman came down in favor of an employer mandate. This approach had the advantage of expanding coverage significantly without increasing taxpayer expenditures. This was particularly important in light of the tremendous increases in spending for Medicare and Medicaid during the 1980s (Health Care Financing Administration 1996 p. 189, Table 1). However, there were at least two major drawbacks. First, the employer mandate would leave a large number of individuals without coverage; *i.e.* it was an incomplete solution. Second, there was concern that employers would pass the full cost of coverage onto employees, leaving workers, particularly low-wage workers, with a pay cut or even jobless. In spite of its drawbacks, Kennedy and Waxman's Basic Health Benefits for All Americans Act of 1989 featured an employer mandate. In addition, they proposed achieving universal coverage through a new joint federal and state program that would cover the unemployed uninsured.

In academic circles, debate ensued over a variety of approaches to expanding coverage. Professor Alain Enthoven of Stanford University joined with his colleague, Richard Kronick, in proposing managed competition. Their plan combined an employer mandate with economic incentives to enhance the competitiveness of the market for health insurance by using a sponsor, a knowledgeable purchaser of health benefits, as the agent of the consumer in transactions with health plans (Enthoven and Kronick 1989). Professor Uwe Reinhardt of Princeton University advocated a mandate requiring individuals, rather than employers, to purchase health insurance (Reinhardt 1989). A coalition of physicians dubbed themselves "Physicians for a National Health Program" and joined the discussion. Their proposal involved combining payers (insurance companies and government payers) into one government payer that would set global budgets for hospitals and pay physicians on a salary or fee schedule basis (Himmelstein and Woolhandler 1989).

While the U.S. Congress and other interested parties discussed different pathways to universal coverage, Massachusetts had already passed the legislation necessary to achieve that goal. The Massachusetts Health Security Act of 1988 extended coverage to approximately 600,000 Massachusetts residents who were not covered by private or public insurance (California Senate Office of Research 1988). The plan centered around an employer mandate, and created new programs with state subsidies to cover anyone not insured through the mandate (Massachusetts Health Security Act of 1988). In California, Senate Majority Leader Barry Keene and Chairperson of the Senate Health and Human Services Committee Diane Watson distributed the Senate Office of Research analysis of the Massachusetts act. In the accompanying letter of June 23, 1988, they encouraged fellow senators to consider a similar approach: "Hopefully, Massachusetts's accomplishment will serve as the model for California as it debates ways to extend health care coverage to its uninsured and underinsured residents."

In California, the generalized concern with the growing number of uninsured was sharpened by a study released in 1988. E. Richard Brown and his colleagues at the School of Public Health at UCLA showed that the number of uninsured Californians had increased from 3.5 million, or 17.4 percent of the nonelderly population, to 5.1 million, or 21.1 percent, between 1979 and 1986 (Brown et al. 1988). While half of that difference was associated with growth in California's population, the other half was attributed to decreasing levels of insurance coverage. California's uninsured rate was higher than the national rate in both 1979 and 1986, but it had also increased at a faster rate: While the national rate had increased two percentage points, from 13.7 to 15.7, California's rate had increased from 17.4 to 21.1, almost four percentage points. California's vast population meant that those percentage points translated into enormous numbers of uninsured individuals.

Insurers Smell the Coffee

As more attention focused on the access issue, the image of the insurance industry in California became increasingly negative. Carriers were seen as entities focused solely on profit-making. Stories emerged of insurers that accepted insurance premiums until an enrollee became costly, and then canceled the policy (Olszewski and Tuller 1990; Tuller and Olszewski 1990). The term "job lock" became a familiar phrase[3] (Garrison 1991). Many insurers refused to cover entire industries, from used-car dealers to government-financed nonprofit organizations (Freudenheim 1990b). A number of insurers simply canceled policies en masse after experiencing losses, leaving thousands — including pregnant women about to deliver — uncovered with little notice (Russell 1988; Tuller 1989). All these activities were perfectly legal, but they outraged and frightened the public.

California's health insurance companies, represented by the Association of California Life Insurance Companies (ACLIC),[4] formed the Uninsured Task Force, which met regularly throughout 1989 and 1990 to explore avenues for change. In addition to redeeming themselves in the eyes of the public, the insurers favored expansion of health care coverage simply because it would increase the volume of insurance sold. Since ERISA[5] motivated many businesses, particularly large firms, to self-insure, many of the carriers' contracts had shifted from fully insured policies to administrative services only (ASO), or simply ended altogether. ASO services provide revenue for the insurers, but the real profits reside in fully insured products. Therefore, the employers who continued to purchase fully insured products, mainly small employers, had become increasingly important. Making health insurance accessible and affordable to this population became a central objective of insurers.

Another cause for alarm among health insurers, in addition to image problems and shrinking profits, was the California ballot initiative on automobile insurance that passed in the fall of 1988. The initiative, Proposition 103, rolled back auto insurance rates by 20 percent (Freudenheim 1990a) and alerted the carriers that something similar could occur in the health insurance industry. An excerpt from a letter from Carl Schramm, then the president of the Health Insurance Association of America (HIAA), to HIAA's board of directors on July 25, 1989, reads: "I wanted you to be well aware of the Association's activities and concerns in California. Proposition 103 was a successful consumer-driven anti-insurance initiative. The potential for the same phenomenon to happen again, aimed this time at health insurance, is real. It has been our assessment that the best avenue to prevent such a measure is to meet and negotiate in good faith with the legislative leadership, employers, providers, and the Health Access coalition."

The Health Access coalition to which Schramm referred was a consumer advocacy group that was working on a tax-financed universal health care initiative with the eventual objective of placing it on the ballot if legislative change did not take place to expand access for the uninsured. Health Access proposed creating an overall budget for all health care in the state, and then subdividing this overall budget by setting global budgets for hospitals and capitation rates for health plans. Providers could choose to practice independently, rather than joining a capitated health plan, but their rates would be set by a fee schedule. Individuals could join prepaid plans or go to the independent providers, but they would have economic incentives to join the plans (Health Access of California 1990). The state would become the funnel through which all health care delivery dollars flowed, and the health insurance industry would play a much smaller role as the market became less competitive and more regulated.

The threat that the carriers faced was that Health Access would use the initiative process to create a government-run health insurance program that would essentially end the private health insurance industry. Carriers began to think that their very survival was at stake, and that they would be best served by coming up with, or at least participating in, a solution to the access issue that left the industry.

AB 350 and the Task Force

In 1989, Assembly Speaker Willie Brown brought Emery (Soap) Dowell, a well-known lobbyist, out of retirement and teamed him up with Steve Thompson, the director of the Assembly Office of Research, to write a bill expanding coverage of the uninsured. The powerful Brown presided over the 46 Democrats who held the majority in the 80-member Assembly; first elected to the Assembly in the early 1960s, Brown had held the speakership since 1980. The core of Brown's bill was an employer mandate. But requiring employers to offer health insurance to their employees would do little to increase access for the high-risk groups that were often either rejected altogether or offered exorbitant premiums for coverage. Implementing the mandate, particularly for small employers, would require reforms in carriers' rating and underwriting practices. Thompson and Dowell asked the carriers for a proposal that they could consider incorporating into the bill. The carriers not only had extensive expertise in underwriting and rating issues but their cooperation would greatly increase the chance of the bill's passage and successful implementation. However, in mid-1989, when carriers were asked for their input, they did not have a proposal prepared. Accordingly, ACLIC (including member company Blue Cross), Blue Shield, and Kaiser Permanente began to meet periodically in an attempt to design a reform proposal that would satisfy both the different carriers and the legislators.

After months of negotiation, the carrier coalition produced the "A and B" approach. The idea was that some carriers, designated "A", would be subject to strict rating rules (through the federal HMO Act or state regulations) approaching community rating, and these carriers would absorb full risk. By contrast, "B" carriers would function as partial risk entities. They would have more underwriting and rate-setting flexibility, and they would participate in a reinsurance pool. The "B" carriers would cede their highest risk individuals and groups to the reinsurance pool, and those carriers would be assessed a percentage of premiums to fund the pool. "A" carriers would not be subject to assessment. All carriers participating in the small group market would accept guaranteed issue and renewal requirements unless limitations on capacity prevented the enrollment of new business; in this case, such carriers would be prohibited from enrolling large groups as well. This proposal recognized the different characteristics and capabilities of carriers — "A" carriers were likely to be large HMOs and service plans, capable of managing the full risk of small groups; "B" carriers were likely to offer indemnity or preferred provider products and to be more skilled at underwriting than at risk management.

While the carriers were developing their proposal, Thompson and Dowell wrote Assembly Bill (AB) 350 for Speaker Brown, who introduced it in mid-1989. The bill required employers with at least five employees to provide health insurance, and also established underwriting reforms. Another bill that would expand coverage, AB 328, was proposed by Assemblyman Burt Margolin, the chairman of the Assembly Insurance Committee. AB 328, a play-or-pay system for universal coverage, was supported by Health Access.[6] Margolin's plan would create a 12-member California Health Plan Commission that would sell subsidized coverage to low-income uninsured Californians (Salzman 1989). Speaker Brown's AB 350, which did not expand the role of the government in the health insurance business, was seen as the more conservative bill and therefore the bill most likely to be signed by Governor Deukmejian. However, as the 1989 legislative session came to a close, the legislators received signals from the governor that AB 350 would not be signed. Preferring some progress to none, Brown converted the bill into a study of covering the uninsured in California. The Secretary of Health and Welfare, Cliff Allenby, and the Secretary of Business, Transportation, and Housing, John Geoghegan, headed the task force. Meetings involved a variety of interested parties, including the insurance industry, the provider community, consumer representatives, and employer groups. The carrier coalition presented their A and B proposal to the task force as a way of ensuring that all employers who were required to purchase insurance would have access to affordable coverage.

In March 1990, the task force released its final report. The outcome of the months of meetings was a recommendation for an employer mandate that was even more comprehensive than AB 350 because it did not exempt employers with fewer than five employees. In addition to the employer mandate, the report proposed expanding California's Medi-Cal system to allow low-wage workers to buy in.[7] It also included the carrier coalition's A and B proposal. A number of participants in the task force opposed the final report. The National Federation of Independent Businesses (NFIB), Health Access, and the California Medical Association all expressed doubt that the plan could expand coverage among the uninsured by relying on Medi-Cal, a publicly run program widely perceived as underfunded and inefficient, without additional funds and cost control measures (Olszewski 1990). Governor Deukmejian did not endorse the final report.

The Focus Shifts to Small Group Market Reform

In spite of the governor's lukewarm reception of his task force's report, interest among the task force participants in addressing access for the uninsured continued. The 1990–1991 legislative session was an active one for health issues, with a number of different bills introduced. Three of the four key bills fell squarely into the employer mandate arena or into the publicly financed health insurance camp. Speaker Brown, following the recommendations of the AB 350 task force, proposed a mandate for all employers to cover workers and their dependents. State Senator Ken Maddy introduced a play-or-pay bill that, like Brown's AB 350 of 1989, applied to employers with five or more employees. In addition, State Senator Nick Petris, in conjunction with Health Access, introduced a single-payer system funded by payroll taxes on employers and employees and integration of the Medi-Cal program. A fourth bill, Assemblyman Baker's AB 4196, was modeled on 1990 Connecticut legislation that enacted changes to underwriting and rating reforms without attempting to significantly expand coverage to the uninsured. The proposal would guarantee issue and renewal, create a reinsurance pool, and limit pre-existing condition exclusions to 12 months. The reinsurance pool, governed by a board of carrier representatives, would create a bare-bones benefit package designed to increase affordability.

None of the four bills introduced in the 1990–1991 session made it through the legislature. During the 1991–92 legislative session, much of the action shifted to the area of small group reform. Efforts to enact comprehensive coverage for Californians continued; they consisted largely of the reintroduction of old bills. Senator Petris and Health Access introduced another single-payer tax-financed delivery system bill. Assemblyman Margolin introduced another version of play-or-pay. But three new bills pertaining to small businesses — SB 1060, AB 2070, and AB 755 — focused attention on issues of underwriting and rating reform.

One reason for increased attention to small group reform may have been the state of California's economy in 1991. California was moving into a recession. The unemployment rate in California for 1991–1993 was 8.9 percent, the fourth-highest rate in the country and much higher than the national average of 7.2 percent (Silverman et al. 1995). During the year ending March, 1991, the state lost 240,000 jobs (Kershner 1991). Governor Pete Wilson, elected in November 1990, inherited a $3.6 billion budget deficit, only to see it revised upward to a stratospheric $7 billion (Block 1990; Scott 1996). The two main options for comprehensive reform — an employer mandate and a tax-financed health care system — both carried heavy economic burdens. An employer mandate threatened job loss, as the forced provision of health care benefits raised wages beyond affordability for some employers. A tax-financed system would surely require a hefty tax increase if universal coverage were to be attained; worse, the ever-increasing costs of medical care promised to require additional increases in future years. By contrast, small group market reform could improve access for some and respond to some of the most egregious problems in the health insurance market without costing the state additional money or threatening jobs.

Before elaborating on the specifics of the various pieces of legislation and the coalitions that formed to support and oppose them, an overview of the major players participating in the debate and the key issues that arose may prove useful.

The Players

The two main groups involved in discussions of California's small group reform proposals were insurance carriers and state officials, with some participation by insurance agents. The carriers were a diverse group, with three main subsets: East Coast carriers such as Aetna, Travelers, Prudential, Cigna, and Metropolitan; the California-based insurers, particularly Blue Cross, Blue Shield, and Pacific Mutual; and the HMOs, led by Kaiser Permanente. There was some overlap, since many of the East Coast carriers and some of the California-based insurers also operated HMOs. The insurance agents were represented by the California Association of Life Underwriters (CALU) and the California Association of Health Underwriters (CAHU).

In the state Capitol, one legislator in particular was heavily involved in the issues. Burt Margolin was the chairman of the Assembly Insurance

Committee and a Democrat with a strong commitment to health care reform. During the early stages of the access debate, he held out for comprehensive reform based on an employer mandate. When it became clear that Governor Wilson opposed a mandate, he began to seriously consider more incremental reform. His chief aide, Lucien Wulsin Jr., was also strongly committed to reform, and coordinated negotiations over the legislation with a liberal agenda.

The Managed Risk Medical Insurance Board (MRMIB) was also a force in the small group market developments. An agency created to administer the state's insurance pool for high-risk "uninsurables," it was staffed by knowledgeable and active participants in the reform process. John Ramey and Sandra Shewry had helped draft the AB 350 Task Force Report while at Health and Welfare; they joined the Managed Risk Medical Insurance Board as the executive and deputy directors, respectively. Lesley Cummings, a staffer on Margolin's Assembly Insurance Committee who became deputy director for legislative affairs at MRMIB, contributed to the consumer-oriented focus at both organizations. In conjunction with the rest of the MRMIB staff, this team had a major impact on the political process.

Organized groups of providers, such as the California Medical Association (CMA) and the California Association of Health and Hospital Systems (CAHHS), did not play a big part in this debate. The CMA chose to focus on broad expansion of coverage through an employer mandate rather than incremental changes to the existing system. Health Access, the consumer advocacy group, viewed small group reform as too insignificant to merit serious attention and continued to push for a comprehensive tax-financed system.

The obvious constituency for small group market reform was small employers and their employees, but economic uncertainty restrained their enthusiasm. Employers wanted increased availability of affordable insurance. However, in an environment of medical care costs increasing at 15 percent per year, avoiding higher taxes and mandates that could further increase costs was even more important (Lehrman 1992). Employees wanted health benefits, but not at the price of reduced wages or job loss. Further, small employers had no real voice in the process. Small employers often belonged to the California Chamber of Commerce, but in the area of health care the chamber was dominated by insurance agents and brokers. For at least two reasons, agents were much more interested in the chamber's health insurance activities than were other types of small employers: first, health care policy directly affected their livelihoods; and second, they understood the issues. The complexity of the health care delivery system presented a significant barrier to involvement of busy entrepreneurs.

The Issues

The central issues in the debate over reform of the small group market were application of guaranteed issue, rating, pre-existing condition exclusions, group size, reinsurance, and employer purchasing pools. This discussion focuses on the views of the insurance carriers, the California Association of Health Underwriters (CAHU), and MRMIB.[8] Numerous interviews and extensive document review indicate that the perspective of the legislative personnel who were involved in the debate are well represented by the position of MRMIB.

Virtually all interested parties supported guaranteed issue for small employers, meaning that every small employer (however that was defined) would be able to obtain a health insurance policy or join a health plan upon request. Insurers would not be allowed to reject any small employer due to existing health conditions, past claims history, or any other reason. The applicability of guaranteed issue, however, was more contentious. Should a small group be allowed by law to purchase any policy on the market, or only designated benefit packages?

Guaranteed Issue

One approach is requiring that insurers guarantee issue of one or two products, which are made available to all comers. Carriers can sell any other product design they wish and deny coverage to high-risk individuals for those products. Some carriers, primarily the insurers based on the East Coast, believed that this was sufficient, since it would ensure that all groups that wanted insurance had access. These carriers were concerned that if they were forced to sell all products to all comers, their rates could rise substantially for healthy groups, who would then be likely to drop insurance. Those who preferred an all-product guarantee, primarily the California-based insurers, claimed that guaranteeing fewer than all products left the system open to gaming. Allowing insurers to choose which products to guarantee issue encouraged them to design thin benefit packages that would be undesirable to the groups most likely to take advantage of the provision. Standardizing the products would eliminate much of this opportunity for gaming by removing control over benefit design from the insurers. However, even with standardized benefits, the one or two products that insurers sold to all comers would enroll the sickest groups over time because those groups would be unable to obtain any other policy. Healthier groups, by contrast, would have access to lower rates on non-guaranteed products. Rates would gradually increase for guaranteed products in an adverse selection spiral that would leave the policies unaffordable. Both CAHU and MRMIB supported guaranteed issue; MRMIB, but not CAHU, specified that it should apply to all products.

Group Size

What size employers should qualify as small groups? The carriers all agreed that going down to individuals and groups of two would leave them open to adverse selection, since decisions were made on an individual basis at that level. But above two, it wasn't clear exactly what number of employees represented an adverse-selection threat. It was assumed that as long as the reforms included guaranteed issue and rating restrictions, they would result in increased premiums for the healthier groups, since the sicker groups that had previously been excluded would now have more affordable access. The debate was over whether a minimum of three employees might result in a significantly greater premium increase for healthy groups than would a minimum of five; the smaller the employer group, the more individually based is the decision whether to obtain coverage. The more individually based the coverage decision, the more likely the decision is made based on anticipated use of medical services. CAHU advocated including individuals and groups of up to 100 employees, beginning with groups of 5–50 and phasing in the expansion over time. MRMIB took the position that the ideal group size was 1–100 but that in no case should the minimum size be more than three or the maximum be less than 50.

Rating

A number of controversial issues also arose around rating practices. There was general agreement that rating restrictions were crucial, since the guaranteed-issue requirement was meaningless without restrictions on rating. But choice of case mix adjusters and width of the rate bands were open to debate. The HMOs supported community rating or very narrow rate bands, while other insurers wanted much broader flexibility with rating. Community rating or narrow bands would shift the focus from underwriting and risk selection, skills at which the indemnity insurers excelled, to utilization management, skills at which the HMOs claimed competitive advantage. To support their positions, each side focused on a different aspect of the likely impact of community rating on the market: HMOs emphasized that community rating would increase affordability for high risks, while the indemnity insurers claimed that it would increase premiums too much and cause large numbers of employers to drop insurance. Both predictions were valid, and the actual outcome could not be foretold with accuracy.

One of the biggest debates was over the factors that would be allowed to adjust the rates. There was general agreement that geography, benefit design, age, and family size were acceptable adjusters. There was much less agreement on industry or occupation, gender, claims history, and health status. A related discussion took place over whether adjustments would take place "outside" or "inside" the rate band. If adjustment was "outside" the rate band, then the insurer could change rates by an unlimited amount, while "inside" adjustment had to occur within the constraints of the rate band. For example, if geography and benefit plan design were outside the rate band and health status were inside the rate band, then each product that had a different geography and benefit plan design combination could have a completely different set of rates, with unlimited variation. However, the rates for each of those combinations could vary with health status by no more than the amount allowed by the rate band. CAHU advocated limiting "outside" adjustment factors to age, family status, and geography. Occupation and health risk adjustments would be limited by rate band constraints. MRMIB favored a similar approach — a limited number of rating factors outside a rate band.

Pre-Existing Condition Exclusions

The HMOs would have preferred that pre-existing condition exclusions be eliminated altogether, since those HMOs that were federally qualified already operated under these conditions. From their perspective, forcing all other insurers to similarly eliminate pre-existing condition exclusions would level the playing field. However, the other insurers feared adverse selection — that employers would move in and out of the health insurance market depending on whether they or their employees had a particular need at the time. CAHU proposed a nine-month exclusion for the first year, decreasing to six months for the second and subsequent years. MRMIB recommended no more than a six-month exclusion for pre-existing conditions.

State Reinsurance

The key issue for reinsurance was whether it would be voluntary or mandatory for small group insurers. Reinsurance essentially ameliorates insurers' incentives for risk selection by allowing them to offload their riskiest individuals and/or groups. For many insurers, it was an essential part of any package that included guaranteed issue. Reinsurance ensured that even though insurers were forced to accept all comers, including the worst risks, they would not be forced to absorb all the costs of care because they could cede those risks to the reinsurance pool. Those who supported the pool tended to be skilled at underwriting, and therefore able to sort out their worst risks upon enrollment and cede them to the pool immediately. By contrast, HMOs had comparatively little skill with underwriting because they focused on absorbing full risk through capitation. HMOs that were federally qualified, which included all those with contracts for accepting Medicare risk enrollees, could impose no pre-existing condition exclusions. This meant that their underwriting skills were somewhat crude — they had a sense of what conditions were so risky as to make an individual uninsurable because they did underwrite policies for individuals but were not experienced at pricing out different conditions. Kaiser Permanente felt that mandatory reinsurance would penalize those carriers able to assume risk, and would force those carriers to gain and use underwriting expertise.

CAHU took no position on this issue except to urge that any state-run reinsurance pool should be designed to maximize choice of carriers. MRMIB endorsed a state-sponsored reinsurance pool, providing that insurers only be allowed to cede groups, not individuals, to the pool. The concern with permitting individuals to be ceded to the pool was that this would result in a reinsurance pool comprised entirely of uninsurables, almost ensuring that the assessments on the participating insurers would be inadequate to cover the costs of the enrollees. If, by contrast, the insurer was forced to cede the entire employer group, then the high-risk individual or individuals in the group would be somewhat offset by the low-risk members of the same employer group.

Purchasing Pools

The concept of purchasing pools was a particularly contentious one. Kaiser Permanente was the strongest proponent of the pools, claiming that they had the potential to decrease administrative costs, lower rates, and expand choice by transforming a group of small firms into a collective with the purchasing expertise of a large firm (Permanente 1991).[9] However, many other carriers opposed the pools, in part due to fear of extensive government involvement. ACLIC, for example, felt strongly that if employer pools were established, the private sector should control and operate them and that a wide variety of plans should be offered (Association of California Life Insurance Companies undated). An even stronger objection to the pools than government involvement was the disturbance to the existing agent-based distribution system in the small group market that such pools would likely entail. Two groups opposed the pools on this grounds: agents, for fear that their role in the distribution system would be undermined; and carriers with well-established relationships with those agents, who foresaw a devaluation of their investment in the agents.

The California Association of Health Underwriters issued a position paper rebutting the idea that employer pools would produce marketing cost savings by eliminating agents:

> Doing away with agents will not eliminate the questions and problems consumers face. Answers and solutions must be provided. If agents are removed from the system, bureaucrats will have to fill the void. This merely replaces the variable cost of commissions with the fixed costs of salaries. Further, consumers are undoubtedly better served by independent advocates and counselors dependent on consumers for their income through commissions than by salaried employees of the same organization from which consumers are seeking redress. Yet small employer pooling mechanisms are targeted at the very businesses too small to afford in-house employee benefits specialists and therefore are the enterprises which rely most heavily on agents.
> (California Association of Health Underwriters 1991b).

Some carriers, including Blue Cross and Blue Shield, had invested heavily in building a distribution structure around the agent-employer relationship, an investment that yielded a strong presence in the small group market. A pool that allowed other carriers to access the small group market without going through the traditional agent distribution system could severely erode the value of their investment. In particular, Blue Cross had close ties to general agents, agents that serve as intermediaries between carriers and brokers. These ties would likely be of little value in a state-run purchasing pool.

Another objection to small-employer pools was that they were unnecessary. CAHU's position paper noted that "private sector pooling mechanisms, namely Multiple-Employer Trusts, already allow small employers to join together to obtain large group benefits at significant savings" (California Association of Health Underwriters 1991b). Rather than initiate a government program to pool small employers, CAHU advocated applying market reforms to the Multiple-Employer Trusts (METs) to ensure that their enrollees would benefit from guaranteed issue and rating restrictions.[10] Blue Cross, in opposing government-sponsored employer pools, cited its own Small Group Access program. This program created an internal Blue Cross pool of small businesses that were rated as one large group. The pool accepted one high-risk group for every four "traditionally accepted" groups, and high-risk groups paid no more than 30 percent more than "traditionally accepted groups (sic) rates" (Blue Cross of California 1991). In addition, claimed Blue Cross, "Passage of carrier reforms such as guaranteed issue will force all carriers to develop other private sector solutions for small groups."

MRMIB supported a state-run purchasing pool in the belief that it would provide choice and stability for small-employer groups. In addition to choice and stability, MRMIB believed that such a purchasing pool could reduce costs by enhancing competition among health plans for pool enrollees, streamlining administration, creating a sponsor with negotiation expertise, and generating volume discounts from carriers.

1991 Small Group Reform Bills

Entering the 1991–92 legislative session, there were significant differences of opinion both among the carriers and between the carriers and the other stakeholders, most notably CAHU and MRMIB. Debate over the numerous bills that were introduced in 1991 — SB 1060, AB 755, and AB 2070 — brought these differences to the forefront.

SB 1060 was a Kaiser Permanente-sponsored measure carried by Senator Ken Maddy, the Republican minority leader. The bill called for a statewide purchasing pool for small employers to be run by MRMIB. According to the Kaiser Permanente proposal, MRMIB would contract with carriers to provide coverage, and carriers would be subject to underwriting and rating requirements. Employees, rather than employers, would select a health plan from the offerings in each area. AB 755 was introduced by Republican Assemblywoman Hansen and backed by Aetna and Travelers. The bill resembled the model bill designed by the National Association of Insurance Commissioners (NAIC), incorporating guaranteed issue of two products and covering groups of 3–25 employees. Carriers could create an unlimited number of separate rate categories for age, sex, family size, and geography. They could also take occupation into account within a 35 percent rate band. For small businesses with similar demographic characteristics (*i.e.*, matched on age, sex, family size, geography, and occupation), rates for the risky firms could still be up to 50 percent more than for the healthy small businesses (California Assembly Insurance Committee 1991; Kaiser Permanente 1991). The third bill, Assemblyman Isenberg's AB 2070, was also modeled after the NAIC legislation.

As 1991 progressed, all three bills stalled in the legislature. Burt Margolin, the chairman of the Assembly Insurance Committee, suggested convening a conference committee on an existing but unrelated bill, his AB 1672. If the carriers could come to an agreement, the agreement could be incorporated into AB 1672 for discussion in conference committee and bypass the legislative bottleneck. This prospect provided the impetus for the carriers to come to an agreement because a united front in the insurance industry would maximize the carriers' influence over the final outcome of the legislation (Association of California Life Insurance Companies 1991c).

In September, after extensive negotiations, the carriers came to agreement on a reform package that could be presented to the AB 1672 conference committee as the insurance industry consensus (Association of California Life Insurance Companies 1991a). All the players recognized the importance of a unified industry stance for an issue that could dramatically affect each organization's way of doing business. The package represented agreement among all the major industry players — ACLIC members (including Blue

Cross), Blue Shield, Kaiser Permanente, the California Association of Health Maintenance Organizations (CAHMO), Aetna, and Travelers. The Eastern carriers (Aetna and Travelers) compromised on stricter underwriting and rating reforms than they had originally proposed in AB 755, and Kaiser Permanente compromised by reducing the state-wide employer purchasing pool to a pilot program in the Bay Area. In spite of a strong preference for an absolute maximum of six months for pre-existing condition exclusions, CAHMO acquiesced to an Aetna proposal for a nine-month exclusion or 60-day waiting period,[11] with a study of the effects of reducing the exclusion to six months or a 30-day wait. Rating methods for geography were also at issue. The Eastern carriers preferred rating by zip code, allowing maximum flexibility, while Kaiser Permanente and the HMOs wanted to divide the state into six regions. The coalition compromised by allowing each carrier to assign separate rates to no more than 58 regions, none of them smaller than a county. The compromise gave the Eastern carriers underwriting flexibility, but the prohibition against splitting a county prevented them from assigning higher rates to specific zip codes.[12]

Although Margolin and the interest groups had hoped to reach agreement in 1991, he decided to postpone convening the conference committee until the 1992 session because the outlook for decisive action in the Senate was unfavorable. Indicating a lack of commitment to the issue, the Senate had waited until the last minute to appoint conferees for the committee, and then had chosen senators lacking strong interest in and knowledge of the issue (Association of California Life Insurance Companies 1991c). Instead of discussing the carrier compromise of September 1991 in conference committee, the consensus package was incorporated into AB 755 so that it could provide a basis for continuing debate of the issues while the carriers waited for the spring 1992 conference committee. However, two major developments unfolded in the interim. First, the carrier community split into two well-defined groups, neutralizing ACLIC. Second, the governor released a small group reform proposal indicating his stand on the issues.

In November 1991, CAHMO withdrew its approval of the carrier compromise. CAHMO had always opposed a nine-month pre-existing condition exclusion; longer exclusion periods conferred greater disadvantage on HMOs because those plans tended to use no pre-existing condition exclusions at all. However, CAHMO had gone along with the nine-month clause rather than hold up the entire package. Now, with no major activity in the legislature, CAHMO decided that it could not support any exclusion longer than six months. Further, CAHMO wanted separate rules for health plans that did not use any pre-existing condition exclusions at all. CAHMO believed that such plans were at a disadvantage in a guaranteed-issue environment in competition with plans that excluded pre-existing conditions, and wanted provisions to help offset adverse selection. CAHMO suggested that plans that did not use pre-existing condition exclusions be allowed to guarantee issue to groups with minimum size five instead of three; be allowed to temporarily cease enrollment of small groups when a "target enrollment" had been reached; and be exempt from guaranteed issue if they could prove that they had experienced adverse selection (Association of California Life Insurance Companies 1991b; Association of California Life Insurance Companies 1992a).

In January 1992, CAHMO reached an agreement with the other carriers. Pre-existing condition exclusions were limited to six months, and an annual target enrollment for small groups of 6 percent of the carrier's prior year enrollment was established for all carriers (not just those that chose not to use pre-existing condition exclusions). Carriers that reached their target could stop selling policies in the small-group market, but would not be allowed to re-enter the market for the rest of the year (Association of California Life Insurance Companies 1992a). This meant that the "Eastern carriers" of AB 755, led by Aetna and Travelers, were united with the California HMOs; the fact that a number of the Eastern carriers, such as Prudential and Cigna, had major HMO operations and belonged to CAHMO helped the agreement. The compromise was incorporated into AB 755. Although this agreement appeared to reunite the industry behind one package, the real split was yet to come.

The Blue Pacific Coalition

Several carriers had always been somewhat dissatisfied with the extent of the agreed-upon underwriting and rating reforms. Blue Cross, Blue Shield, and Pacific Mutual led this group, which also included New York Life and Employer's Health Insurance. These carriers had tried to place their concerns on the table for discussion, first by requesting amendments to AB 755, and then by introducing AB 2070. But their attempts to amend AB 755 failed, and AB 2070 died. A two-day meeting was held in January 1992 with the objective of reaching consensus among the factions, but efforts at compromise failed. These carriers acknowledged the importance of a united industry; the greater the degree of consensus, the stronger the industry's voice in negotiations with policymakers over the final outcome. However, the faction decided that their objections were strong enough to justify splitting off and creating their own piece of legislation.

The new bill, AB 3657, was introduced by Assemblyman Horcher and sponsored by what became known as the "Blue Pacific" coalition. Several key issues distinguished this bill from the consensus bill, AB 755. Perhaps most important, the bills differed with respect to the application of guaranteed issue. In AB 755, as in the NAIC model bill, insurers were required to guarantee issue of a standard and a basic product. Other design packages could be sold at the discretion of the carriers, who could reject applicants at will. The "Eastern carriers," concerned that relinquishing too much control over their underwriting tools would endanger their survival in the market, favored this approach. They had grown accustomed to risk-avoidance strategies in a market that rewarded skilled underwriters, and were reluctant to see their competitive advantage eroded.

The Blue Pacific coalition preferred an all-products guarantee for two reasons. First, they were dubious that the reforms would be effective in an environment in which any products could be denied to the highest risks. If the only products that the highest risks could access were the standard and basic products, then those were the products that they would purchase. But if all the highest-risk groups were purchasing those products, the premiums for those products would inexorably increase, leaving the products undesirable for anyone who had access to another product with a lower premium, namely the healthy groups. The potential for the "death spiral" of adverse selection was obvious. But with guaranteed issue of all products, insurers were forced to take all comers for any policy that they sold, which in theory would lead to a more even spread of risks across products. Equally important, the Blue Pacific coalition believed that all-product guaranteed issue would give them a competitive advantage. First, it would run the shady carriers out of the market. These carriers would habitually enter a market, offer extremely low premiums, and enroll a large percentage of the small employers in an area. Then, they would observe each employer's claims experience over time, dropping the costly employer groups. They succeeded through dumping the bad risks and retaining the good; they lacked skill at managing risk, and excelled only at avoiding it. If these carriers were forced to guarantee issue and renewal of every policy they sold, they would no longer be able to avoid risk and would likely exit the market. Second, Blue Cross and the other carriers knew that underwriting was one way to manage risk (primarily through avoiding it), but they believed that there were other methods that would be equally effective, such as utilization control. They believed that a more sophisticated marketplace, one that restricted the crude risk-avoidance forms of underwriting, would give them an advantage by allowing them to use other risk management tools, ones with which they had more experience and expertise than their Eastern competitors.

Also reflecting its position on these issues, the Blue Pacific coalition failed to include either a reinsurance pool or an employer purchasing pool in its bill. These carriers believed that they would be better off without either type of pool because they had a competitive advantage in each area. In the area of reinsurance, the carriers believed that they were capable of assuming full risk for their enrollees; establishing a reinsurance pool would leave them open to industry-wide assessment if assessment of the participating carriers were inadequate to cover costs. The small-employer purchasing pool bypassed their valuable and effective agent distribution system, eroding their marketing advantage against carriers that had not made a similar investment.

Final Negotiations

The Blue Pacific bill, AB 3657, entered the fray in March 1992. The following month, the governor released a proposal for small group reform that re-oriented the debate. Governor Wilson had reiterated his position on the issue of health care reform in January in an interview with the *San Francisco Chronicle*: "As he has in the past, Wilson expressed opposition to any government-paid universal health insurance system and to any requirement that all employers pay for health insurance for their workers. Because of the state's terrible financial shape, any bill entailing huge costs is considered dead on arrival. 'We're not going to do anything that is either wise or good if we impose upon small employers burdens that they cannot afford,' he said. 'And we certainly won't do anything good for the state's competitiveness'" (Gunnison 1992).

Instead, Wilson's proposal endorsed an employer purchasing pool, a state reinsurance pool, and underwriting and rating reforms, including guaranteed issue and renewal (Governor Wilson 1992). From a political standpoint, the proposal sent a clear message that the administration strongly supported enactment of small group reforms, virtually ensuring passage through the legislature. The abrupt upturn in the legislation's likely fate gave fresh energy to industry efforts at compromise; if the legislation were sure to pass, it would behoove the industry to create a consensus that would lend strength to its negotiating position.

As conference committee meetings began, the main proposals on the table were AB 755, AB 3657, and the governor's proposal. The first meeting, held on April 21, 1992, consisted of presentations by four panels of interested parties: the administration, the AB 755 coalition (Kaiser Permanente, Aetna, Travelers, CAHMO), the Blue Pacific coalition (Blue Cross, Blue Shield, and Pacific Mutual), and "Other Interested Parties."

At this point, the legislative staff, administration, and interest groups began to meet regularly in an attempt to hammer out an agreement that would be acceptable to all. Lucien Wulsin Jr., Assemblyman Margolin's chief aide, organized and facilitated these meetings. Wulsin would gather the groups together with an agenda of items to be discussed. Participants in these meetings recall them as long, frequent, and sometimes frustrating but also productive. The conference report was signed by all but one of the conferees on August 26; Assemblyman Isenberg, the lone dissenter, held out for inclusion of individuals and groups of two in the reforms and refused to sign the report. AB 1672 was then approved by the Assembly and the Senate, and was signed by Governor Wilson in September 1992.

Outcome

The final version of the legislation featured stronger reforms than either of the proposed bills. In Table 2.1, the first column shows the parameters of AB 755 as it was revised in March 1992. The second column shows the Blue Pacific coalition's bill; the third displays AB 1672 as it was passed and signed in August and September 1992. In each area, AB 1672 went at least as far as the stronger of the two proposed bills, and in several areas it exceeded both bills. The final bill adopted the AB 755 definition of group size, 3–50 employees, starting at 5–50 and phasing in the expansion over two years. It applied guaranteed issue to all products as advocated by the Blue Pacific

TABLE 2.1   Comparison of Small Group Legislative Packages

	AB 755 (as amended 3/92)	AB 3657 (as amended 4/92) (Blue Pacific)	AB 1672 (final version)
Supporters	Kaiser, Aetna, Travelers, CAHMO	Blue Shield, Blue Cross, Pacific Mutual	
Group Size	3–25 / 3–50	5–25	5–50 4–50, starting 7/94 3–50, starting 7/95
Application of Guaranteed Issue	standard and basic products; applies only to group size 3–25	all products	all products
Guaranteed Renewal	yes	yes	yes

Rating Factors
  Geography
  Age
  Family Size
	up to 12 regions
	7 categories
	4 categories
		up to 12 regions
		7 categories
		4 categories
			up to 9 regions
			7 categories
			4 categories

Rate Band Width	+/–30%	+/– 30%	+/– 20% +/– 10%, starting 7/96
Pre-Existing Condition Exclusions	One time limit: 6 months for 5–50 9 months for 3, 4	One time limit: 6 months	One time limit: 6 months
State Reinsurance	yes	no	yes
Employer Purchasing Pool	yes, pilot program in the Bay Area	in concept	yes, state-wide program

Sources: AB 1672 Conference Committee (1992); Association of California Life Insurance Companies (1992c); California Senate Insurance, Claims and Corporations Committee (1992); California Statutes (1992).

Coalition, rather than just standard and basic. The carrier proposals agreed on guaranteed renewal, rating categories for age and family size, and the grace period for continuous coverage when switching between jobs; AB 1672 simply adopted these provisions. However, carrier agreement was not sufficient for adoption into the final bill: AB 1672 was more hard-hitting than either bill with respect to geographic rating factors and rate band width, allowing a maximum of 9 rating regions for statewide carriers and restricting rate band variation to +/-20 percent, dropping to just 10 percent in 1996. Both carrier proposals had advocated up to 12 geographic regions for rating, and plus or minus a full 30 percent in the rating band. Following the governor's lead, AB 1672 adopted provisions for both a reinsurance pool and a purchasing pool, expanding AB 755's Bay Area pilot program to a state-wide pool run by MRMIB.

The Failure of Comprehensive Reform

For the liberal legislators and staffers who were working to pass AB 1672, the small group reform package was considered a first, and quite minimal, step toward comprehensive reform that included universal coverage. An ACLIC memo from April 1992 describes the first conference committee on AB 1672:

> Chairman [of the Assembly Insurance Committee] Burt Margolin, in his opening remarks, indicated that he viewed the reforms as phase one of a more comprehensive, universal health insurance approach. He seemed to be seeking an undefined linkage or commitment between action on small group reform this year, and a comprehensive bill next year.
> (Association of California Life Insurance Companies 1992a)

California's Insurance Commissioner, John Garamendi, shared Margolin's view:

> . . . I want to emphasize that the small group underwriting and rating reforms now being considered are intended only to correct certain egregious problems in the insurance marketplace. Our work in this area should not be viewed as the centerpiece — or even a major part — of the more comprehensive health care reform that we so desperately need in California.
> (Garamendi 1992)

The sweeping changes advocated by Margolin and Garamendi did not materialize. While the debate over small group reform continued throughout 1991 and most of 1992, a number of global reform measures were introduced. The California Medical Association, which had chosen to focus on comprehensive reform based on an employer mandate rather than devote resources to the small group effort, sponsored bills in both the Assembly (AB 2001, Brown) and the Senate (SB 248, Maddy) and put Proposition 166 on the November 1992 ballot. Insurance Commissioner John Garamendi, with help from his advisor Walter Zelman (who went on to become one of President Clinton's chief health policy advisors), proposed a universal coverage system featuring managed competition. Each of seven regions would have its own health alliance; automobile, workers' compensation, and health insurance would all be rolled into a single 24-hour coverage plan. Garamendi's proposal was drafted as a study rather than an implementation bill, and was introduced in the Senate as SB 6 (Torres) and in the Assembly as AB 502 (Margolin). Senator Petris appeared once again, with Health Access again as a sponsor, again advocating a Canadian-style single payer with SB 308.

Unlike AB 1672, none of these measures made it through the legislature and the governor's office. Proposition 166, the CMA's employer mandate, was defeated soundly, opposed by almost 70 percent of California's voters. Both an employer mandate and a tax-financed single-payer system had now been rejected on numerous occasions, and were not likely to be seriously considered again soon. California's budget woes could not have helped. The 1992 elections followed a summer of struggling with the ballooning deficit, the state's "worst budget crisis in its history" (Paulson and Zeiger 1992 p. 425). The increasing severity of the recession further reduced tax revenues, and expenditures for services for education, welfare, and the prison system continued to grow. The completed budget was 65 days late, forcing the state to issue IOUs in lieu of payroll checks. The final budget cut deeply into health, welfare, and education programs, but preserved funding for the Department of Corrections (Paulson and Zeiger 1992).

This excerpt from an ACLIC memorandum in early 1992 describes the environment at the time: "California's treatment of the health access issue has progressed to near total agreement that universal access must be assured, politically and as a social objective. However, achieving this objective through a government run system or an employer obligation (pay-or-play, mandate) is probably not viable in California in 1992. A distracted legislature and sagging economy will not permit enactment of universal approaches to expand public and private health insurance coverage" (Association of California Life Insurance Companies 1992b). Instead, Californians advocating comprehensive reform turned their attention to the national stage, where newly elected President Clinton promised global reform for the entire nation.

Implementation

Both of the key components of AB 1672 — the rules and the purchasing cooperative — went into effect on July 1, 1993. The implementation phase of the rules was relatively straightforward, with much confusion but only one major controversy: application of the rules to trade association health plans. The purchasing cooperative implementation was more involved because the legislation delegated significant flexibility to the Managed Risk Medical Insurance Board to design the program and make the key decisions. The following discussion begins with the implementation of the rules, focusing on the trade association issue. The discussion then moves to the start-up phase of the purchasing cooperative, the Health Insurance Plan of California (HIPC), emphasizing the evolution of MRMIB's policies on the role of insurance agents in the HIPC. Some observations on the results of each component of the reform are briefly noted.

Rules

> AB 1672 may be the most dramatic single piece of health insurance regulation legislation yet enacted in California in terms of the fundamental changes it makes in the insurance market to which it applies. Unfortunately, it also teems with ambiguities and uncertainties, many of which could be exploited by some segments of the insurance industry in order to evade the Act's requirements and frustrate the Legislature's intent in enacting the law. . . The existence of such problematic language is demonstrated by the flood of inquiries which this Department has received since the legislation was signed in the Fall of 1992.

So begins the Department of Insurance June 11, 1993 notice of proposed emergency regulations pertaining to the implementation of AB 1672

(California Department of Insurance 1993b). In response to the confusion over interpretation of AB 1672, the department issued four sets of emergency regulations and five bulletins between April 1993 and October 1994. Questions to which the Department of Insurance responded include the following (California Department of Insurance 1993a):

- Are "supplemental coverages" such as "cancer" subject to AB 1672?
- What happens if a 3–50 employer adds or loses employees and ceases to be a "small employer" as defined in AB 1672?
- If a carrier declines to participate in the small-employer market under AB 1672, may it continue to renew small-employer coverages issued prior to the effective date of the new law?
- In applying the standard employee risk rates, is geographical region based on the location of the employee's residence or the employer's principal place of business?
- What happens to previously excluded employees or dependents on July 1, 1993?

Insurance Commissioner John Garamendi, well known for his consumer orientation, interpreted the legislation in a manner in keeping with the "intent of the Legislature" as put forth in the law:[13]

> It is the intent of the Legislature in enacting this act to guarantee the availability and renewability of health insurance to small employers, to prevent abusive rating practices, to require disclosure of rating practices to purchasers, to establish rules for continuity of coverage for employers and covered individuals, to improve the efficiency and fairness of the small group health coverage.
> (California Statutes 1992 Chapter 1)

In spite of confusion over the specific requirements of the regulations, their substance was relatively non-controversial. One reason might be the high degree of penetration of managed care in the California market. In the U.S. in 1993, HMO penetration was at 22 percent and PPO/POS penetration was at 20 percent (Health Insurance Association of America 1995 p. 26).[14] By comparison, 36 percent of Californians were enrolled in HMOs and 38 percent in PPOs (Health Insurance Association of America 1995 pp. 44, 48). Thus, managed care market share — HMO, PPO, and POS products — was at 42 percent for the nation and at 74 percent for California in 1993. Managed care focuses on cost containment through managing and reducing utilization, skills that would likely be rewarded with market share in California's reformed small group market. In California, unlike in states with less experience with managed care, many insurers were familiar with these skills and were ready to compete on the newly leveled playing field.

Associations

The most impassioned and prolonged implementation battle generated by the regulations was over the application of the new law to trade and professional associations that included small employers. Participants in the negotiations agree that if the issue of exemption of professional associations from the requirements of AB 1672 had arisen earlier, it could have killed the entire reform package. As it was, the insurance industry's late realization of the implications of AB 1672 for trade association business resulted in four years of negotiations, culminating in legislation passed and signed during the 1996 session.

Many trade and professional associations offer health insurance to their members as one of the benefits of joining the association. Often some, but not necessarily all, association members are employers in the 3–50 size range. AB 1672 required that if any small employers that offered health insurance to their employees were among the participants in the association's health insurance plan, the carrier issuing insurance to the association must abide by all the small group rules (Eowan 1993). The legislation had implications for at least three groups. Any carrier that had been dealing with associations as large-group business and that had no other small group business would have to either become a small group carrier or give up the association business. Any association that had been receiving a health insurance product tailored for its members with better-than-average rates would experience increased premiums, at least for its small group members; carriers were no longer allowed to offer them deals that were not available to the small group market in general.[15] These two groups were unhappy about the unforeseen effects of AB 1672, and advocated association exemption from AB 1672 to continue the status quo. Finally, associations with a combination of individuals, small employers, and large employers as members would have to sort out which rules applied to whom; the AB 1672 reforms selectively protected their small group members while leaving their individual members, groups of two, and groups of more than 50 employees without the small group guarantees.

AB 1838, introduced in 1993, proposed to exempt associations from the AB 1672 rules by allowing carriers to selectively offer coverage to associations. Under AB 1838, carriers would be able to sell health insurance packages to some associations but not to others, and to sell insurance to associations without having to guarantee issue to the entire small group market. This would have satisfied both the carriers whose only small group business was through association members and associations accustomed to receiving favorable rates and products. But supporters of the small group reforms feared that such legislation would remove a large chunk of the relatively low-risk small group market from the reforms and allow carriers to continue to segment the market by selectively marketing to low-risk associations (Managed Risk Medical Insurance Board 1993).

AB 1838 was the first real test of the commitment of the legislature and the administration to small group market reform, and the supporters of reform mobilized against it. Along with MRMIB, numerous government agencies and private organizations registered opposition, including the Health and Welfare Agency, the Department of Insurance, Consumers Union, the California Medical Association, and several insurers. Kim Belshe, the deputy secretary of the Health and Welfare Agency, was quoted in the *Sacramento Bee* as saying that she had "'extremely serious concerns about the Costa bill in its present form, and would strongly urge the governor to veto it'" (Jacobs 1993). AB 1838 passed in the Assembly but, in spite of the efforts of various trade associations, failed in the Senate Committee on Insurance, Claims, and Corporations.

The other association problem — selective applicability of AB 1672 to the membership of associations — was addressed by AB 2059 and AB 28, which were both passed and signed during the 1993 session. AB 2059 (Margolin) and its cleanup companion expanded AB 1672 to apply to all members of "guaranteed associations." A guaranteed association was defined as one that had continually provided coverage to its members since 1987 and that consisted of at least 1000 members. Thus, an individual who is a member of a guaranteed association receives the same protections as a group of 3–50, even though an individual outside the association does not. Further, all members of such associations are allowed to join the HIPC, regardless of the size of their employer group.

Most of the trade associations were satisfied with AB 1672 and its amendments. But the issue was not yet resolved: The Senate Committee on

Insurance, Claims, and Corporations considered AB 1838 once again, in July 1994. The struggle of 1993 was repeated, with a similar lineup of opponents on each side and another round of letters and editorials. This time, however, support for the bill was narrowed because AB 2059 and AB 28 had removed some of the bill's constituency: "Despite vocal and dire claims by numerous associations in support of the bill during 1993, only three associations actively promoted AB 1838 in 1994. The others had been able to obtain acceptable coverage in the general small group market even without the ability to strike special deals unavailable to the general small group market" (California Department of Insurance 1994). The bill again failed to emerge from the committee, but the battle was not yet over.

During the 1995 session Assemblyman Knowles introduced a new bill, AB 1360. This bill was sponsored by the two remaining associations that were vocally dissatisfied with the effects of AB 1672 — the California Bankers' Association (CBA) and the California Society of Certified Professional Accountants (CSCPA). Members of both associations had experienced increased premiums as a result of AB 1672 (Harman 1995; Turner 1995). Under AB 1672, compression of rates meant that the groups that had been receiving the lowest premiums due to their favorable risk status would experience the largest increase, just as those with the highest rates would observe the largest reduction. The CBA and the CSCPA had long been receiving premiums that represented significant discounts from the standard rates. Thus, while many associations observed negligible increases, stable rates, or decreases, the CBA and CSCPA saw their rates rise substantially. The increase was essentially a redistribution from the relatively low-risk association members to the small group market at large; whether this redistribution was unfair or long overdue was a matter of perception.

The new bill exempted qualifying associations from AB 1672, and was so narrowly written that only the CBA and the CSCPA qualified. Although AB 1360 did not pass in 1995, an amended version was passed and signed in the 1996 session. This bill does not exempt the associations from the AB 1672 requirements. However, it does permit them to receive a discount from carriers for performing administrative functions that would otherwise be the responsibility of the carrier, such as premium collection. To prevent the discount from becoming a loophole allowing carriers to offer preferential treatment to low-risk associations, the discount must be offered to every guaranteed association that performs the same administrative functions.

Thus, the CBA and the CSCPA receive no preferential treatment. It remains to be seen whether this compromise will put the issue to rest permanently.

The battle over associations was a significant one because association exemption could have seriously weakened the reforms by allowing an exit for low-risk small employers. For redistribution from low-risk employers to high-risk employers to work effectively, the low-risk employers must not be allowed to circumvent the reforms; although they are not required to purchase insurance, neither can they obtain it without submitting to the rules of the market. Yet an association exemption would have created exactly the alternative pathway to insurance that would allow low-risk employers to retain insurance but escape the new market rules. The strong opposition to the association exemption bills on the part of policymakers and other interested parties — including a number of insurers — demonstrated firm commitment to upholding the principles of small group market reform.

Results

Surveys performed before and after the implementation of the reforms show that the number of firms providing health insurance to their employees in the small group market rose between 1993 and 1995 (Buchmueller and Jensen 1996). The largest increase was in the smallest size category: The percent of employer groups of size 3–24 providing coverage increased from 58.7 percent to 64.7 percent. The increase for firms with 25–49 employees was much smaller — 82.8 percent to 83.3 percent — but from a larger baseline. The increase in coverage cannot be directly attributed to the passage of AB 1672, but comparison to coverage rates in the small group market outside California indicates that the legislation was at least a contributing factor (Buchmueller and Jensen 1996).

Studies of the first post-reform year performed by the California Department of Insurance (DOI), charged with overseeing fee-for-service plans and PPOs, and the California Department of Corporations (DOC), responsible for "health care service plans" (HMOs), demonstrated that the transition to a reformed marketplace had been relatively smooth. The DOI found that "the carriers reported the feared problems with adverse selection had not yet materialized, predatory pricing was not a problem and, for the short term, competition may have increased" (Turem, Executive Summary). The DOC commented that "the fact that more insurers are competing for a share of this market segment may be contributing to the persistent downward pressure on rates that most companies are reporting" (California Department of Corporations). Further, employers seemed to fare reasonably well under the new regulations: "The breadth of the allowable 'rate bands' appears to have been sufficient to permit a relatively smooth transition to the new environment for most affected employers. However, a few groups with unusual demographic characteristics experienced significant rate increases" (California Department of Corporations p. 8). The emphasis on managing risk may have encouraged increased participation by HMOs in the small group market. The Department of Insurance noted that the fee-for-service plans and PPOs had lost approximately 10 percent of employer groups and 5 percent of lives over the first post-reform year, while the Department of Corporations recorded a 22 percent gain for HMOs in small group market enrollees (Turem; California Department of Corporations).

A survey reported by Buchmueller and Jensen (1996) found corroborating changes for the period immediately following implementation of the reforms. Table 2.2 shows a dramatic increase in the number of small employers whose primary health plan is an HMO or POS plan and a corresponding

TABLE 2.2   Health Plans Offered by Employers With 3–49 Workers

Primary Health Plan	1993	1995
California Firms		
Conventional	25.5%	4.0%
HMO/POS	42.4	62.2
PPO	29.8	27.6
HIPC	—	2.8
Other/Don't Know	3.3	3.4
Firms Outside California		
Conventional	72.8%	35.1%
HMO/POS	12.9	39.5
PPO	14.3	25.4
HIPC	—	—
Other/Don't Know	—	—

Source: Buchmueller and Jensen (1996), Table 2, p. 28.

decrease in the number whose primary plan is conventional coverage. A comparison cohort of non-California firms show a similar trend of replacing conventional coverage with HMO and POS plans, although California's firms start from a baseline of greater managed care penetration.

The Health Insurance Plan of California

Following the signing of AB 1672 in September 1992, the Managed Risk Medical Insurance Board was charged with implementing the purchasing pool component of the legislation. The proposed start date was July 1993, giving MRMIB just nine months to make a large number of policy decisions regarding the structure of the pool, to issue regulations, and to market the new pool to potential enrollees. In spite of the short time-frame, the HIPC's start-up period was relatively smooth. The program enjoyed broad support from Governor Wilson, who took time to undertake a "high-profile campaign" promoting the HIPC as a way for employers to pay "wholesale rather than retail prices" (Russell 1993a). From Wilson's perspective, the pool had a number of advantages: it was voluntary, it aided small business, and it avoided taxpayer expenditure. It also soon became apparent that the pool had the potential to serve as a proving ground for the health alliances that were the building blocks of Clinton's health plan, bringing a national policy spotlight to California.

MRMIB's implementation plan was designed to minimize bureaucracy and streamline the start-up process. One key decision was to contract out the daily operations of the program, tapping the efficiency and experience of the private sector and allowing MRMIB to function with an internal staff of just 13.[16] The vendor selected for operations, Employers Health Insurance, is a large insurance company with expertise in marketing and enrollment. The MRMIB staff also took advantage of existing expertise and information. For example, the geographic boundaries for the new HIPC were adopted from those already in operation for the state high-risk pool. The initial approval of plans applying for inclusion in the HIPC used Department of Corporations approval — known to be stringent — as evidence that a plan had a sufficient delivery network in a given geographic area.

The specifics of the issues debated and the decisions made in the process of getting the HIPC up and running were relatively uncontroversial. Two sources provide information in these areas. Lipson and De Sa (1995) discuss the development of policies related to enrollment and premium collection, participation rules for employers and employees, health plan participation requirements, boundary issues, and defining a uniform benefit package. Buchmueller (1996a) reviews the decision to restrict participation to managed care plans, the development of standard and preferred benefit packages, criteria for plan participation, and geographic boundary determination. These issues, while interesting, created little conflict and are more relevant to a discussion of purchasing cooperative design and implementation than to a political history. Rather than duplicating discussion of these issues, the next section focuses on an area of policy creation and implementation that was controversial and that has been less discussed: the role of insurance agents in the HIPC.

Agents and Added Value

The HIPC's approach to agents has resulted in problems with agents, difficulties with carriers, and may be one reason that the HIPC's growth has fallen short of expectations. Changes in the HIPC's policy reflect growing acknowledgment of the role that agents play in the small group market and increased efforts to accommodate them.

The initial structure of agent compensation through the HIPC reflected the perception that agents contributed little value to the insurance transaction. At least two factors contributed to this perception. Managed competition, the theoretical framework for the HIPC's design, provides no role for agents. In addition, the debate over health care reform at the national level focused on Clinton's developing plan, from which agents were notably absent. As a result, the enrollment process was designed to make agents optional, under the assumption that many small firms would forgo their services and save the commission if given the opportunity. Those employers who chose to use an agent to help with enrollment paid the agent a HIPC-set fee, which was itemized separately on the employers' monthly premium bill. Rather than using the traditional percentage commission, the HIPC adopted a flat fee mechanism that varied with group size. Flat fees separate the agents' remuneration from the characteristics of the firm's employees, so that agents do not receive larger commissions for placing older groups with higher premiums in the HIPC. For a group with fewer than 25 enrollees, the monthly agent fee was $50; this went up to $75 for a group of 26–50 and

$100 for a group larger than 50.[17] In addition, employers paid a $4 fee for each enrollee on a monthly basis. During the second and subsequent years, the $4 per-enrollee fee remained in effect but the group fees did not (Health Insurance Plan of California 1995–96). Employers who did not use an agent checked a box on the application form to indicate as much and avoided paying the fees.[18]

Agents and carriers had a number of problems with this structure. Carriers, notably Blue Cross and Blue Shield, use general agents as a cornerstone of their distribution systems. General agents serve as middlemen between carriers and agents, providing assistance to agents with quotes and enrollment for the carriers that they represent. They are compensated by the carriers for this service. The HIPC included no compensation provisions for general agents at all. This was a major factor in the initial refusal of Blue Cross and Blue Shield to participate in the HIPC. Agents, for their part, were unhappy with three aspects of the payment scheme: the relatively low fees, the optional use of an agent, and the disclosure to the employer of the agent fees in the monthly bill. Blue Shield, in a letter of April 6, 1993 to its agents, linked its refusal to join the HIPC to its displeasure with the HIPC agent policy: "Although we believe that the concept of a pool in state and national health care reform is most likely a long-term reality, Blue Shield of California cannot support a pool which does not acknowledge the value of the agent and broker community to small employers in their selection of health care programs."

One industry executive provides a perspective that was repeated in a number of interviews.

> The HIPC made sense conceptually, but its organization did not because it tried to bypass the agents and brokers. Agents and brokers have long been the distribution channel for the small group market, aside from Kaiser Permanente, and insurers generally use agents rather than a captive sales force. AB 1672 ignored this market phenomenon, in part due to the national reform campaign taking place in 1992. On the national level, brokers and agents were perceived as cost without value, and it was assumed that cutting them out of the chain would result in net gain. The HIPC adopted the national view, and assumed that if they cut the agents out, the HIPC would sell itself. The HIPC has been seen as antagonistic to the broker community from Day 1, and the brokers coalesced against the HIPC. The HIPC won't realize its potential growth until it either manages to legislate brokers out of existence, or learns to embrace them.

The collapse of the Clinton plan has ended contemplation of an agent-free small group market. Just as important, although employers were given the option of joining the HIPC directly and saving the agent fees, the vast majority chose to go through an agent and voluntarily pay the fees, indicating that small employers perceive value in the services agents provide. These two factors have contributed to the recognition that agents are a crucial link to small firm enrollment, and the HIPC has increasingly moved to accommodate agents. A compensation scheme treating agents more favorably began on July 1, 1996. The agent fee is still itemized separately on the employer's monthly bill, but now the employer must pay the agent fee regardless of whether enrollment occurs through the HIPC staff or through an agent. In addition, the first-year commissions are now higher, although the per-enrollee fees have remained at $4.[19] The new fees can amount to a significant increase in compensation. For some group sizes, such as 21–25 and 41–50, monthly payment for the first year of enrollment has doubled. In addition, whereas agents previously received only the $4 per enrollee fee after the first year, now they receive the monthly commissions as well (Health Insurance Plan of California 1996–1997).

In addition to the changes in compensation structure, the HIPC has undertaken outreach efforts in an attempt to increase agent involvement in the program. In July 1995, the HIPC introduced the Agents of Choice (AOC) Program. The AOC Program rewards agents for selling the HIPC with "lead calls" — cold calls that the HIPC telemarketing staff makes to small employers in the zip code of the agent's choice. The program offers 100 lead calls in exchange for agent enrollment of three cases or 60 employee lives. During its first year, the AOC Program staff made more than 15,000 lead calls to employers on behalf of agents (Health Insurance Plan of California 1996). Another development was a newsletter, *Choicewords,* introduced in January 1996 to provide "news and information from The Health Insurance Plan of California." The newsletters include information on HIPC commissions, profiles of participating agents, and surveys requesting information to help the HIPC improve services to agents and their client employers.

Some insurance agents like the HIPC, but others have little use for the program. Those who like it cite ease of comparison due to the standard benefit package, outstanding service from the HIPC's administrative contractor, absence of underwriting (the rates in the program brochure are the exact rates, with no variation), and the AOC Program for referrals. Even those who don't like the HIPC admit that it is difficult to beat its selection of health plans. One agent who sells frequently through the HIPC admits that the fees are low but sees the HIPC as a way to "get in the door with clients" and sell more profitable products, such as life insurance and 401K plans.

The HIPC's relationship with the agent community continues to evolve. The HIPC is currently considering "burying" the agent fee in the premium. The HIPC would no longer separate out the agent fee from the premium and administrative sections of the employer's monthly bill. Agents strongly favor this, and for this reason it could enhance HIPC growth. However, before adopting this practice, the HIPC must come to terms with whether this would too greatly compromise the HIPC philosophy of full disclosure of agent fees. The HIPC's desire to expand through tapping the major "retail" outlet for health insurance — agents — clashes with its long-held belief that agents add little value to the health insurance marketplace. In its efforts at reconciliation with the agent community, the HIPC seems to be acknowledging the agent's central role in the distribution of health insurance. But until the HIPC's perception of the agent's value is favorably revised — recognizing not just the agent's necessity but the agent's worth — the tension that characterizes the current relationship will remain unresolved. The future growth of the HIPC may depend in part on the resolution of this tension.

Results

The HIPC began operations with tremendous publicity, widespread support from the governor, and lofty expectations for enrollment — MRMIB hoped to sign up 10,000 people per month and to reach 250,000 in two years (Russell 1993b). The reality has been more moderate, but steady, growth. The first year concluded with 54,000 and the second year with approximately 91,000 enrollees (Brown 1996; Lipson and De Sa 1995). Growth has proceeded more slowly since the end of the second year; enrollment figures did pass the 100,000 milestone but not until well into 1996. At the end of March 1997, HIPC enrollment totaled 124,215 employees and dependents from 6,647 firms.

Enrollment has amounted to a small percentage of the potential target market of all small employers in the state. One reason is that many small employers simply are not interested in purchasing insurance: low profit margins, high employee turnover, the high cost of insurance, and administrative hassles are some of the reasons frequently given (Hall and Kuder 1990; Lippert and Wicks 1991). Many employers who do provide insurance are satisfied with their current carrier and are uninterested in making a switch.

Approximately 20 percent of HIPC enrollees were previously uninsured, a not insignificant number, but hardly one that makes a noticeable dent in California's uninsured population. Although the HIPC has had little impact on the number of uninsured in California, some evidence suggests that it has helped intensify competition in the small group marketplace, lowering premiums for small firms. The Department of Corporations first-year report on the results of the reforms credited the HIPC with contributing to the pressure to lower premiums in the small group market at large: "The introduction of the HIPC, its standardized plan designs, and the general premium decrease at the July 1994 renewal are factors intensifying the drive toward

TABLE 2.3   Monthly Premiums for Employee-Only HIPC Plans

	1993–1994	1994–1995	1995–1996
Standard HMO			
mean	$131.90	$117.33	$110.83
range	$102–162	$95–144	$92–153
number of plans	64	78	88
Preferred HMO			
mean	$145.48	$130.17	$123.67
range	$118–176	$110–163	$107–166
number of plans	64	79	88
Standard PPO			
mean	$136.31	$130.37	$151.75
range	$97–195	$102–195	$112–184
number of plans	18	18	10
Preferred PPO			
mean	$150.01	$143.31	$169.36
range	$106–208	$111–204	$123–202
number of plans	18	18	10

Source: Buchmueller (1996b), Table 1.

lower premiums" (California Department of Corporations p. 7). Table 2.3, from Buchmueller (1996b), presents composite premiums for employee-only plans in the HIPC. Premiums declined for all four types of plans from the first year to the second. For the third year (1995–1996), HIPC premiums have continued to decline for the HMOs but have risen for the PPO plans.[20] Whether the HIPC can continue to hold down premium increases for HMOs in coming years remains to be seen.

Market Forms of Alliance

The HIPC has proven to be a moderately successful way to unite small employers for the purchase of health insurance — although it has fallen somewhat short in enrollment, it has exceeded expectations with respect to holding down premiums. But must the HIPC be run by a government agency? Why couldn't a private entity do as good a job, or even better? Indeed, why was the HIPC needed in the first place when multiple-employer trusts and associations performed much the same tasks? Isn't it the case that forcing the associations to abide by the AB 1672 rules disadvantaged at least some of them, raising premiums for their members who would have been better off without the new law? Before discussing these questions, it is useful to distinguish between two issues: first, whether private-sector alliances of small businesses are a viable form of organization; second, whether such alliances should be subject to the rules of the market in which they operate.

Consider first the private-sector issue. Few would argue that private-sector alliances are inherently bad. Many private purchasing pools for small employers operate throughout the country, some of them dating back many years. One of the most frequently cited examples is the Council of Smaller Enterprises (COSE), established by the Cleveland (Ohio) Chamber of Commerce in 1973. COSE, a private nonprofit entity, enrolls firms with up to 150 employees and currently serves approximately 200,000 enrollees (General Accounting Office 1994). Indeed, the HIPC itself is slated for privatization. AB 1672 contains a provision requiring that MRMIB issue a request for proposal for nonprofit entities to take over the HIPC. The first RFP, issued in 1996, generated no response, most likely due to the $3 million start-up debt that MRMIB is still repaying for the HIPC. A second and final RFP will be issued in 1997.

Privatization of the HIPC, if it does go through, need not be a poison pill. In the words of one individual involved with MRMIB and the HIPC:

> The advantage of privatization is elimination of the bureaucracy associated with state agencies, such as rules governing hiring and purchasing and restrictions on travel. Opportunities which could make the HIPC more attractive, such as combining the current plan coverage with workers' compensation coverage, are difficult to pursue from within the government because decisions are based on politics instead of the market. Such a plan would upset the competition, which would go to the Legislature to object, and the end result would likely be that the HIPC would be prohibited from entering the workers' compensation market. The disadvantage of privatization is that association with the state gives the HIPC stability and credibility that were crucial to its success. Those advantages, however, were more or less front-loaded, so that ties to the state are less important now that the HIPC has proven itself a success.

To the extent that the disadvantages of government involvement outweigh advantages over the long term, it may be in the best interests of the HIPC to pursue privatization.

The key issue is not whether private is good or bad but whether there should be any constraints on the form of private-sector alliances. Should alliances operate within a regulatory framework, or should they be allowed to take any form their creators design, assuming some baseline protection against fraud? MRMIB has taken the position that a regulatory framework for private pools is essential, and that it should be strongly purchaser-oriented (Managed Risk Medical Insurance Board 1995). Accordingly, to best serve and protect the interests of the purchasers, private cooperatives should be nonprofit and should be administered by a board that represents purchasers. Board members should be subject to conflict-of-interest provisions to prevent them from compromising the interests of the purchasers. For example, insurance agents and employees of insurance companies should be prohibited from serving as board members. To encourage health plan participation, ensure equity, and prevent excessive dependence of the cooperative on any one health plan, the cooperative should outline objective criteria for participating carriers and contract with multiple plans. To protect quality of care and encourage cost-conscious choice of health plan, cooperatives should offer choice of plan at the employee level and hold an annual period of open enrollment during which all employees may switch plans.

MRMIB's consumer-oriented perspective is not the only approach to purchasing cooperative design. A variety of frameworks have emerged from the states that have passed purchasing cooperative legislation (Alpha Center 1996; Institute for Health Policy Solutions 1995; Ross 1995). Ohio has allowed private pools to proliferate, largely free of any regulatory framework. Private alliances in Ohio must be nonprofit and cannot be controlled by the insurance industry, but few other restrictions constrain form or function (Institute for Health Policy Solutions 1995). This approach relies on competition to keep premiums down and to prevent the pool's operators from charging unfair administrative fees. The next section discusses the struggle over the development of a regulatory framework for private-sector alliances in California.

Consider now the rules issue. Should private-sector alliances — loosely defined as including purchasing pools, trade association health plans, multiple-employer trusts, or any other voluntary alliance of small employers that incorporates the function of health insurance purchasing — be exempt from the rules governing health insurance purchasing? This question essentially translates into a question about whether a healthier-than-average subset of the small group market should be allowed to split off to receive preferential rates. Without the market rules, these voluntary associations are free to screen their members, allowing only the healthier-than-average access to coverage. This is a question of values: Those who believe that the well should help subsidize the sick will come down against exemption from market rules, while those who believe that every group should cover its own costs will favor exemption. The battle that was fought between the associations and the supporters of the reforms during the implementation phase of the market rules was over exactly this issue. The members of the associations of bankers and accountants had long been receiving favorable rates, and AB 1672 threatened those rates. The perception of the associations was that they were paying their own way; the perception of the reform supporters was that the associations were unfairly opting out of the larger community of small businesses and avoiding taking on a share of the costs associated with the community's risk. The outcome was that the associations were forced to play by the rules — members can still obtain insurance through the associations, but the associations have been forced to absorb some of the risk of the larger community. Other states have taken other paths (General Accounting Office 1995). In Vermont and New Hampshire, association plans are allowed to negotiate a separate community rate for their members that is not tied to the rest of the market. In Montana, associations that guarantee issue to their members are exempt from the market rules.

California Choice

The regulatory framework for private alliances has been developing on two parallel paths in California: one legislative and one regulatory. Much of the action has been on the regulatory front, initiated by Word and Brown, a general agent firm in Southern California.[21] Word and Brown ignited controversy in 1995 when its owners applied for a license from the Department of Corporations to operate an organization that would contract with carriers and small employers to facilitate the sale and purchase of health insurance. The organization, called California Choice, would function as a for-profit enterprise.

The Department of Corporations approved California Choice in January 1996 without citing its rationale, leaving the Department of Insurance to wonder what criteria the DOC had employed when evaluating the application. An excerpt from a February 1996 letter from Republican Insurance Commissioner Chuck Quackenbush, who replaced Democrat John Garamendi in the November 1994 elections, to the commissioner of the Department of Corporations, reads:

> It would appear that a precedent has been set as to how health alliances should be established and that subsequent creation of new products may be stifled . . . I am extremely interested in obtaining information from the DOC that supports your decision to approve California Choice. I have not yet seen regulations or a DOC bulletin on the subject, so I am assuming that this was a decision based on your regulatory authority as commissioner. I would appreciate whatever information that you could provide to my office.

Although it is unclear what standard the DOC used for evaluation, it may relate to the distinction that Word and Brown made between a marketing cooperative and a purchasing cooperative in their application. A marketing cooperative is defined as a group of sellers gathering together to offer products to buyers, while a purchasing cooperative is a group of buyers gathering together to purchase products from sellers. While a purchasing pool run by the insurance industry on behalf of employers might have difficulties with conflict of interest, a marketing pool run on behalf of agents and carriers would have no such problems; it would simply be another way to sell insurance. Regardless, California Choice is now up and running. In addition to governance, at least one other feature distinguishes the private-sector alliance from the HIPC: it can be accessed only through insurance agents (BNA's Managed Care Reporter 1996).

On the legislative front, the latest development is the passage and signing of Senate Bill 1559 during the 1996 legislative session. This bill legalizes private pools and allows them to be run as for-profit entities. However, conflict-of-interest provisions are required, which means that the insurance industry will be prohibited from operating the pools. Word and Brown claim that the law does not apply to California Choice because it is a marketing and not a purchasing pool. Efforts are underway to pass legislation that would force the DOC to reveal the basis upon which it granted approval to California Choice. Now that it is clear that for-profit industry-run purchasing cooperatives are prohibited, more agents can be expected to turn to the path that Word and Brown took.

The Potent Combination of Policy Entrepreneurship and Anxiety

Policy proposals sometimes wend their way through the legislative process and emerge as law in spite of the apparently insurmountable obstacles that confront them. One set of circumstances under which a policy proposal would be expected to fade away even before reaching the stage of serious consideration is characterized by well-organized prospective opponents and unmobilized beneficiaries. Marmor et al. (1981) call such an uneven political contest, with concentrated interests on one side and diffuse interests on the other, an imbalanced political market.[22]

> The incentives to press claims for concentrated interests are much greater than those for diffuse ones. The prospect of having one's well-being greatly affected creates substantial incentives to act to protect one's interest. An interest marginal to one's well-being — even though large when aggregated over the class of affected parties — provides weak incentives to act. This distribution of incentives results in a systematic imbalance of the probabilities of interest representation. . . The theory of imbalanced interests holds that concentrated groups, other things

being equal, will be more effective in the political process than diffuse ones. (Marmor et al. 1981 p. 147)

Marmor and his colleagues use their framework to support their claim that the government is unlikely to undertake effective action to hold down medical inflation. The more likely the government policy is to be effective, the less likely it is to be enacted because effective policy incurs concentrated costs on providers, who will mobilize to defeat it.

Yet sometimes policy is enacted even when one side experiences concentrated costs and the other experiences diffuse benefits. What are the conditions under which these obstacles to policy — a mobilized opposition and an unmobilized constituency — can be surmounted? James Q. Wilson suggests one contributing factor: the role of policy entrepreneurs as substitutes for the unmobilized constituency of the policy. Wilson has presented a framework similar to that of Marmor et al. for relating the likelihood of mobilization to the concentration of costs and benefits (1973). He has also created a typology to characterize the regulatory politics that emerges from different contests (1980). When costs are concentrated and benefits are diffuse, the politics is "entrepreneurial." Those who would benefit from the policy have little incentive to organize because rewards are too small, but those who would be hurt have a strong incentive to mobilize. Often, the interest group wins and kills the measure, but "policy entrepreneurs" sometimes take on the interest group on behalf of the public: "The entrepreneur serves as the vicarious representative of groups not directly part of the legislative process" (Wilson 1980 p. 370). Ralph Nader, perhaps the best-known policy entrepreneur, has successfully mobilized public sentiment to pass regulations on automobile safety and clean air.

Kingdon (1995) has described policy entrepreneurs as idea or proposal advocates that may be found within government or outside it, in academia or in interest groups: ". . . their defining characteristic, much as in the case of a business entrepreneur, is their willingness to invest their resources — time, energy, reputation, and sometimes money — in the hope of a future return" (p. 122). They may have a variety of motives: pursuing personal interests, as in the case of a politician interested in demonstrating effectiveness that can be cited during a re-election campaign; promoting their values, as in the case of national health insurance advocates; or simply an enjoyment of the process — some "simply like the game" (p. 123). Whatever their position and motivation, policy entrepreneurs can sometimes push policy proposals along in lieu of activity on the part of the real constituency.

Even when policy entrepreneurs arise on behalf of inactive beneficiaries, their activity may not be sufficient to push through a policy that is opposed by powerful interest groups. In this case, the threat of major change can make the difference by shifting the perspective of the opponents. When some degree of adverse change appears inevitable, organizations may decide that their resources can be better used in attempting to influence the degree and the terms of the change rather than in trying to defeat it altogether. "Sometimes organized interests are able to ameliorate the extent of a defeat; an apparent loss thus masks the degree to which things would have been worse had the organization not gotten involved" (Tierney 1987 p. 97). Thus, when health care reform (temporarily) appeared inevitable under President Clinton, interest groups focused on asserting influence on the specifics of the legislation (Skocpol 1994).

When dramatic change poses a serious threat to the status quo, one approach for potential opponents is to influence the terms of the proposed change; another is to suggest or support an alternative proposal that pre-empts the larger one. In this case, a proposal that would otherwise have been fought instead receives support. Rather than viewing a policy proposal as antithetical to their interests, fear of far-reaching change may cause potential opponents to see it as acceptable, even congruent with their interests to the extent that it pre-empts the dreaded alternative. Relatedly, the success of the policy proposal will be maximized if it is incremental. Much of the analysis and decision making regarding policy alternatives is performed in an incremental fashion (Kingdon 1995; Lindblom 1959). However, the incremental nature of policies is particularly salient when the support of a proposal is tied to the defeat of a more comprehensive alternative. The more far-reaching the proposal, the more it is likely to resemble the dramatic change that the opponents fear, and the more likely they will be to mobilize against it.

The next section discusses the passage of small group market reform as a specific case of the general situation described above: the combination of policy entrepreneurs and the looming threat of comprehensive national reform allow the passage of legislation that would otherwise have failed due to well-organized opponents and inaction on the part of unmobilized beneficiaries. Although no policy would be expected to result from such a situation, small group market reform emerged. Policy entrepreneurs from various branches of government became involved on behalf of the small employers. After answering the first question posed at the outset of this chapter — how the policy passed at all — the discussion moves on to the other two questions: explaining the relatively far-reaching nature of the legislation and its sustainability. The chapter concludes with a brief comment on future prospects for the reforms.

Overcoming Obstacles to the Passage of Small Group Market Reforms

Potential Opponents Instead Take Pre-emptive Strike at "Canada"

The insurance community was well positioned to mount a strong struggle against small group market reforms, with several lobbying organizations at the ready. The two most important were ACLIC and CAHMO, both staffed by experienced personnel in Sacramento. They understood the issues thoroughly, no small matter in dealing with the complexities of health care coverage and its regulation. And they had the motivation to oppose the reforms due to their potential effects. An environment of guaranteed issue and rating restrictions would encourage higher risks to enter the market, increasing average premiums. Premium hikes would be steepest for the lowest-risk groups, some of which would drop coverage, reducing the number of insured small employers and causing premiums to rise still farther. In the best-case scenario, premiums would rise only slightly or not at all, and few low-risk employers would exit the market. But in the worst-case scenario, premiums could rise substantially, causing significant exodus from the market and a large reduction in the volume of small group business for insurers.

Even more worrisome was the potential for an uneven distribution of the high risks entering the market. Any insurer that attracted a particularly high-cost group of enrollees would have to continually increase premiums to cover costs; the inability to turn away high-risk groups or charge them their actuarial costs could force an insurer with a particularly costly pool of enrollees into bankruptcy. As the chief actuary of one large insurer put it, small group reform took away the tools that the insurers used to protect themselves, leaving them fearful about organizational survival in a strictly reformed environment.

Given the potential adverse effects of the policy on the insurance industry, mobilization to oppose it might have been expected. However, not only did the industry refrain from opposing the policy, the insurance community actually rallied around it. The key factors predisposing the insurance industry to consider measures that it would otherwise have dismissed or fought was a pervasive sense of the inevitability of some form of health insurance reform and the perceived threat that reform could entail dramatic departure from the status quo.

Extensive media coverage of the enormous and growing numbers of uninsured played a part in creating a sense of inevitability; particularly relevant to the California discussion were the new data produced by Professor E. Richard Brown's study of the uninsured in the state. In response, debate during the 1980s in academic circles and at all levels of government produced a wide variety of approaches to providing health care to all citizens. Some, such as an employer mandate coupled with Medicaid expansion, interfered little with the traditional insurance function. But others, such as the Health Access coalition's Canadian-style proposal for global budgets and fee schedules, contemplated the end of the existing insurance industry. Some type of governmental response to the problem appeared inescapable in the late 1980s, and the insurance industry feared "Canada."

Unattractive as were some of the legislative proposals, equally unattractive was the prospect that government inaction would propel consumer advocates into action. In California, the passage of the 1988 ballot initiative heavily regulating the automobile industry served as a wake-up call for the health insurance industry: Failing to take a proactive stance with respect to some type of health insurance reform could leave the fate of the industry in the hands of the voters. The outcome could be far worse than the insurers might achieve by cooperating in the legislative process.

Under the circumstances, endorsing small group market reform was an attractive option on a number of fronts. Although the reforms would restrict insurers' contracting autonomy and rating flexibility somewhat, they would leave the insurance industry fundamentally intact, which was not to be taken for granted. Importantly, the reforms would affect only small firm business; all other business would be left untouched. Moreover, the changes would benefit many of the insurers. Reform of the market would eliminate many of the shady carriers that had earned the industry negative publicity and a reputation for ruthless profiteering. Increasing accessibility to high-risk small employers would expand the potential market for profitable fully insured health insurance products. Given the alternatives, small group market reform was attractive to the insurers, and their support — in principle, even if they did not always agree on the specifics — was instrumental to its success.

Policy Entrepreneurs Substitute for Beneficiaries

The most obvious beneficiaries of the new rules were high-risk small employers. In the pre–AB 1672 market, high-risk small employers faced high premiums or outright denial of coverage. The new rules would allow them guaranteed access to insurance coverage at reduced rates. The small employer community as a whole would also benefit, although less directly and immediately. The lowest-risk employers would lose the discounted premiums they were receiving, but they would benefit from the security of ensured availability of insurance. Low-risk employers were only a single high-utilization employee away from status as high-risk employers, and the new law would prevent such a case from resulting in steep premium hikes or denial of coverage.

However, small employers did not mobilize. Small employers are a diverse community, with no real connection other than the number of employees in their firms. Some are wealthy partnerships of attorneys and physicians, while others are small mom-and-pop convenience stores. Entrepreneurs tend to be busy, focused on immediate business concerns. Health care coverage is only one of many issues competing for scarce time and attention, and they have no human resources department to which the matter can be delegated for study and action. The prospect of being forced to provide insurance to employees did hit home with small businesses because some of them foresaw a serious threat to their survival. But as long as coverage was not required, they had other priorities. Those employers who could not obtain coverage or found it excessively costly prior to the legislation's passage simply did not provide it; those for whom the cost of coverage rose excessively could always drop it as a benefit.

In the absence of a motivated constituency, a number of policymakers took on the issue and pushed the passage of the legislation. Three groups with diverse agendas converged on the same objective — far-reaching small group market reform. Assemblyman Burt Margolin and his aide Lucien Wulsin Jr., the staff of the Managed Risk Medical Insurance Board, and Governor Wilson all played important roles in the formulation and eventual passage of small group market reforms.

Margolin and Wulsin had originally focused entirely on promoting state-wide universal coverage; several play-or-pay bills, built on an employer mandate, had been introduced to further this objective. However, the passage of any reform at all was not assured, and they eventually concluded that some reform was better than no reform. Once they turned their attention to small group market reform, their impact on the process was significant. Margolin provided leadership in the Assembly, inserting the reforms into his AB 1672 and pushing for the appointment of a conference committee on the bill. Wulsin was a tireless negotiator, working through the details of the various proposals with the different carrier factions, representatives of insurance agents, and MRMIB.

A second important component of the policy entrepreneur coterie was the Managed Risk Medical Insurance Board. The key staffers involved in the reform battle were John Ramey, Sandra Shewry, and Lesley Cummings. Ramey and Shewry had worked for the Health and Welfare Agency under Cliff Allenby; they authored the AB 350 Task Force report that resulted from Speaker Willie Brown's employer mandate bill. Cummings had worked for the Assembly Insurance Committee and its chairman, Assemblyman Margolin. She then teamed up with Ramey and Shewry to staff MRMIB, which was created to run the Major Risk Medical Insurance Program, a tobacco tax-subsidized program providing insurance to high-risk individuals who have been rejected by commercial insurers. All three were well acquainted with the issues, and together they were a formidable advocacy force for reform in the small group market. The MRMIB trio served as the consumer-oriented voice of small employers. As such, they were an advocacy organization within the administrative bureaucracy. They believed that reform would significantly improve the functioning of the small group market by creating a set of rules that all carriers would be required to obey; the purchasing cooperative would provide the added benefit of extensive choice at the employee level. The new market, even if it couldn't significantly expand access, would eliminate the most egregious practices that had prevailed and would improve the situation for some small firms without hurting others excessively. To that end, they pushed hard for restrictive rules, and played a role in enacting relatively far-reaching reforms.

For Governor Wilson, the reforms provided a way to demonstrate concern with the access issue and support for small business at no cost to the recession-plagued state. His key aide in the small group reform issue, Kim Belshe, had worked closely with John Ramey at Health and Welfare. She shared the MRMIB perspective on the value of a reformed small group market, and convinced Wilson that the issue was an important one. Participants in the process agree that without the jump-start provided by Governor Wilson's proposal for small group market reforms, the legislation might have bogged down in endless battles over the details of numerous proposals. His support revitalized the issue and made passage of some form of reform a priority for the legislature. In the words of one participant, "Things were messy and going nowhere for a while, until the governor got involved." Wilson's main effect was to keep the legislation moving, but he also had a major impact on one of the reform provisions — the purchasing pool. When Wilson's reform package included a state-wide purchasing pool, the extensive debate on this point ended.

A Window for Incrementalism

Policy succeeds in part due to chance. Kingdon (1995) perceives the window of opportunity for policy proposals as the convergence of three separate "streams" — a problem that demands attention and resolution, a policy proposal that provides a solution to the problem, and political circumstances that facilitate the enactment of the proposal. In the case of small group market reform, these conditions came together in 1992. The issue of the uninsured and affordable access became a focal point; small group market reform addressed access and affordability for small firms, if not significantly expanding coverage for the uninsured; and policy entrepreneurs converged on the issue to push its passage.

Circumstances changed substantially shortly after the passage of AB 1672. The bill was signed in September 1992 and went into effect of July 1993. By 1994, President Clinton's reform plan had collapsed. Prospects for national reform of the health care system had ended, and so had the insurance community's apprehension of a broad threat to its existence. Legislative and administrative advocacy were also weakened. By the end of 1994,

Margolin and Wulsin had left the Assembly for the private sector. Even if they had remained, the atmosphere in the Assembly was chaotic and unproductive following the 1994 elections, when the Republicans won a majority for the first time since 1970 by just one seat.[23] Governor Wilson had turned his attention to a 1996 presidential bid, and his frequent absences and focus on the national scene distracted his attention from the insurance issue. MRMIB was still a strong force for advocacy, but it seems unlikely that the agency could have pushed the reforms through independently; the convergence of a variety of policy entrepreneurs was the key to their effectiveness.

The policy window that opened in the early 1990s for small group reform allowed room for only incremental change. Interviews with participants unearthed a number of circumstances under which the window of opportunity could have slammed shut before the bill could pass through. One such issue, as has been discussed, was the trade association exemption: If the trade associations and the insurers that dealt with them as large group business had foreseen the impact of AB 1672, they would have killed the bill. Another issue was the request for proposal for privatizing the HIPC: If this provision had not been included in the bill, the agent community would have rallied to quash it due to fears that the purchasing cooperative would cut them out of the distribution system. Also of note is that all of the more comprehensive bills under consideration at the same time in the legislature failed. Although this analysis does not explore the reasons behind the failure of those measures, the fact that each of them failed while small group reform passed is suggestive of the increased likelihood of success when change takes place in small doses.

Extent of the Reforms

Explaining why the reforms that emerged were as restrictive as they were introduces a new factor: the fragmentation of the insurance industry. During the initial phase of the small group reform discussion there were several distinct groupings of carriers, each of which sponsored its own bill in the legislature. But cohesion is one of the most important resources that interest groups bring to bear in their struggle to influence policy outcomes: "Part of a group's stock in trade in affecting all phases of policy making — agendas, decisions, or implementation — is its ability to convince governmental officials that it speaks with one voice and truly represents the preferences of its members. If the group is plagued by internal dissension, its effectiveness is seriously impaired" (Kingdon 1995 p. 52). In acknowledgment of the importance of unity, each faction compromised and produced an industry-wide agreement in September 1991. The compromise, as might be expected, featured moderate rules (neither tight nor loose) and a Bay Area purchasing cooperative (neither state-wide nor nonexistent). But when the legislature did not move on the compromise bill, the coalition fragmented.

More surprising than the fractiousness of the insurance community was that they ever came to agreement at all. Each subset of the insurance community had different competitive advantages and vulnerabilities, and each group advocated a policy outcome that would be desirable for its own position in the market. The Eastern carriers were most worried about losing the underwriting tools that protected them from uncomfortable levels of risk. The Blue Pacific coalition opposed a purchasing cooperative that would bypass its active agent-based distribution system. The HMOs, which generally did not use pre-existing condition exclusions, feared the adverse-selection consequences of competing in a guaranteed-issue market against insurers using the maximum allowable exclusion period. Although they briefly overcame their self-interested pursuit of maximizing their competitive advantages and protecting their vulnerabilities in favor of the greater good, the period of consensus quickly passed.

ACLIC, which had played a major role in earlier negotiations, was immobilized as a political force when some of its membership split off to form the Blue Pacific coalition. This excerpt from a January 6, 1992 ACLIC memo demonstrates that the likely consequences of this fragmentation were clearly understood by the organization (p. 3):

> It became clear at the end of the 1992 legislative year that some legislative staff would attempt to push their agenda well beyond the so-called "carrier coalition" draft and that the CMA and others would also push for restrictive reforms not acceptable to the industry. This atmosphere will continue. It might be effectively overcome by industry unity. Presently the industry is not unified. A divided industry presents at least two extremely unattractive possibilities:
>
> 1. ACLIC is neutralized — open warfare between companies and opposition by other carriers and interest groups leads to an expensive stalemate. The industry's time, political resources and image will be dissipated in contention that ultimately results in preservation of the status quo, but does not silence critics of current small group health insurance business practices.

2. The Legislature, unfocused as it will be, becomes disgusted with the industry turmoil, and works with the Administration and the Department of Insurance to devise a restrictive system no carrier will like.

Either of these alternatives suggests the conclusion that the industry should renew efforts to unite.

ACLIC, fully aware that a unified industry would wield greater influence over the legislation's final outcome, attempted without success to broker a compromise (Association of California Life Insurance Companies 1992d). As predicted by ACLIC, the failure of the carriers to unite around a single set of principles allowed room for consumer-oriented legislative advocates to play a large part in the final outcome.

The result of the work of Margolin and MRMIB was tighter rules than any of the carriers had considered. On each issue, the final bill went at least as far as any industry proposal had gone. Even when the various industry factions agreed on an issue, the final version sometimes went beyond it; this was the case with the number of geographic areas allowed and the width of the rating bands. Margolin, Wulsin, and MRMIB had the thorough understanding of the issues that was crucial to creating their own version of reform, rather than simply going along with one of the proposals put forth by the insurance industry. In the words of an observer, "The insurance companies did feel throttled by John [Ramey], Sandra [Shewry], and Lesley [Cummings], but the divided industry couldn't prevent the outcome."

Sustainability of the Reforms

Reform does not end with the passage of legislation; implementation can present challenges at least as great as those undertaken en route to transforming a bill into law. What were the key obstacles to the implementation of small group market reform and how were they overcome? This question is particularly relevant to contests between parties experiencing concentrated costs and those experiencing diffuse benefits, as in the case of small group market reform. Such circumstances create an opportunity for policy entrepreneurs to enter the fray on behalf of the unmobilized beneficiaries, but the "new, usually temporary, political constituency" may dissipate once the legislation has passed and new challenges distract the entrepreneurs (Wilson 1973 p. 335).

The main threat to the implementation of the market rules was the belated realization of some professional associations that the new law would end preferential treatment by their current insurers. Because the most directly affected associations were powerful business interests with a strong lobby, they posed a serious threat to the integrity of the reforms. The reforms were based on preventing small employers from accessing health care coverage without sharing in the cost of the health risk in the entire community of small employers; the success of the associations in obtaining an exemption would have provided them with an escape route and encouraged others to follow. To date, the associations have not managed to obtain an exemption; their biggest victory has been the allowance of a discount for the provision of administrative services that the insurers would otherwise provide. However, this discount must be offered to any association, precluding the possibility of preferential treatment and making the victory somewhat hollow.

The key factor in combating the threat posed by the associations was the mobilization of small group reform supporters both inside and outside the government. In response to the association problems, Assemblyman Margolin created new legislation resolving the confusion over application of the reforms to associations. His bills satisfied most of the associations, eroding much of the support for the exemption bill. Governor Wilson, despite intense pressure from business interests, held firm in support of small group market principles. Without the strong commitment of the reform advocates, the exemption doubtless would have been granted. Whether it would truly have undermined the reforms cannot be known for certain.

The main political battle over the implementation of the purchasing cooperative has revolved around the role of insurance agents in the cooperative. The HIPC staff, beginning the implementation phase with the expectation that national health care reform would render insurance agents irrelevant, did not befriend the agent community. The compensation structure for HIPC enrollment compared unfavorably with prevailing market remuneration, and employers could easily bypass the agents and avoid their fees by contacting the HIPC directly. The HIPC's early actions played a part in the refusal of some health plans to participate in the cooperative, and earned it some degree of enmity in the agent community.

The collapse of the Clinton plan in 1994 made it clear that insurance agents will not be irrelevant anytime soon. As the HIPC has come to recognize that agents are not just relevant, but central, to the distribution of insurance in the small group market, it has moved to accommodate them by restructuring its compensation system and providing incentives to enroll new firms in the HIPC. The lesson to be learned from the HIPC's evolving relationship with the agent community is the importance of adaptation to changing circumstances. Rigid conformity to ideology that has ceased to be realistic — in this case, the view that agents are dispensable in the small group market — can present just as real a threat to successful reforms as can a political challenge by a strong opponent, such as that mounted by the CBA and the CSCPA over exemption of trade associations from the reforms.

One obstacle that was expected but did not materialize deserves note because of the detrimental effect it could have had on the reforms: premium increases. Because the reforms redistributed some of the financial burden of health risk from the high risks to the low risks, premiums were expected to rise for those who had previously been paying the lowest premiums. Some of those employers, it was assumed, would decide that health care coverage was no longer worth providing at the higher price. If enough of the low-risk employers dropped coverage, prices could rise substantially because the risk level of the remaining employers would be significantly higher. The result could be a net reduction in the number of employers covered, and at higher prices than before the reforms. However, the impact of premium increases on low-risk small employers in California cannot be evaluated because the expected increases were not observed, other than in a few isolated cases and in the two trade associations that voiced objections. In the years since the passage of AB 1672, premiums have consistently exhibited a downward trend as a result of a strongly competitive market, and the anticipated exit of low-risk employers has not occurred.

Future Prospects

Given that the reforms have survived to this point, can we assume that they are securely ensconced in the regulatory framework of the market? Interviews with various reform participants, industry executives, and insurance agents have generated two opposing viewpoints on this question. One perspective is that the small group market reforms are at best in need of defending against encroachment, and at worst are currently unraveling. One respondent suggested that pressure leads to reform, and easing of pressure leads to reversal of reform. Another cited a laundry list of problems with successfully maintaining the reforms over the long run, including the complexity of the issues, the absence of a consumer constituency, the uncooperative stance of insurers now that the threat of more comprehensive reform has faded, and the growing apathy of the administration.

On the other side is the positive effects that the reforms appear to have had on the market to date, and the few negative effects. In interviews, insurance agents tended to be quite happy with the reformed market; one of them described the pre–AB 1672 days as the "wild west." Likewise, insurance executives expressed satisfaction with the reforms. No segment of the insurance community or other interest group appears to be gearing up to derail the reforms; indeed, the reforms seem to have reduced premiums, increased stability, and made the market more competitive. Major issues, including the association exemption issue and the private pool issue, have been resolved with the reforms intact. One politically powerful respondent asserted that the reforms were very solid, and faced no threat of reversal whatsoever.

The negative perspective on the reforms may be overstating the case, but even the positive perspective on the reforms does not extend to expanding them to new populations, such as individuals and the 51–100 employee market. The consensus seems to be that the most that can be expected right now is that the reforms remain intact. Perhaps this is not surprising; after all, the conditions under which small group reform squeezed through the window of opportunity no longer hold in today's market.

Consider the market for individual insurance. Even more than small firms, the individual market for insurance — including the self-employed, the unemployed, individuals transitioning between jobs, and many seasonal workers, among others — is extremely diverse and unlikely to mobilize in favor of reforms. Like the small group reforms, reforms in the individual market would constrain the insurance industry, forcing alteration in current screening and rating practices. Further, the concerns regarding adverse selection and its consequences are much stronger in the individual market. As a result, guaranteed issue of all products in conjunction with rating restrictions is likely to encounter much more resistance. Yet, while the obstacles to reform loom even larger than they did prior to small group market reform, neither the threat of comprehensive reform to bully the insurers into cooperation nor a strong coalition of policy entrepreneurs appear in the picture. Discussion of far-reaching reforms to address the uninsured issue are absent from the national and the state agenda. Margolin and Wulsin are gone. Governor Wilson is unconvinced that reforms in the individual market are necessary or have the potential to be effective. Key staffers have left MRMIB. While these factors do not mean that individual reform cannot occur in California, the current conditions do mean that now is an unlikely time.

APPENDIX:
List of Abbreviations

AB	Assembly Bill
ACLIC	Association of California Life Insurance Companies
ASO	Administrative Services Only
CAHHS	California Association of Hospitals and Health Systems
CAHMO	California Association of Health Maintenance Organizations
CAHU	California Association of Health Underwriters
CALU	California Association of Life Underwriters
CBA	California Bankers Association
CMA	California Medical Association
CSCPA	California Society of Certified Public Accountants
DOC	Department of Corporations
DOI	Department of Insurance
ERISA	Employee Retirement Income Security Act
HIAA	Health Insurance Association of America
HIPC	Health Insurance Plan of California
HMO	Health Maintenance Organization
MET	Multiple-Employer Trust
MRMIB	Managed Risk Medical Insurance Board
NAIC	National Association of Insurance Commissioners
NFIB	National Federation of Independent Businesses
POS	Point-Of-Service
PPO	Preferred Provider Organization
SB	Senate Bill
TPA	Third-Party Administrator

Notes

1 Much of the information presented in this chapter comes from 23 interviews with those involved in the political process, the insurance industry, or both. Interviews took place between June 23, 1995 and April 3, 1997.

2 Minimum group size was subsequently reduced to two employees to bring California into compliance with the federal Health Insurance Portability and Accountability Act of 1996.

3 "Job lock" describes the situation faced by individuals with pre-existing medical conditions who are covered through their employers. Since such conditions are often excluded by a new policy, job mobility and self-employment may be constrained.

4 ACLIC has since changed its name to the Association of California Life and Health Insurance Companies (ACLHIC) to reflect the importance of health insurance to its member companies. ACLIC's membership overlapped with that of the Health Insurance Association of America (HIAA), including such national companies as Cigna, Prudential, and Metropolitan. However, some HIAA companies chose not to belong to ACLIC, notably Aetna and Travelers; others carriers, such as Blue Cross, belonged to ACLIC but not HIAA. To complicate the issue of insurance industry representation, HMOs had their own association, the California Association of Health Maintenance Organizations (CAHMO; now CAHP, the California Association of Health Plans), and there was also overlap between CAHMO and ACLIC.

5 ERISA, the Employee Retirement and Income Security Act, was passed by the federal government in 1974. An unintended consequence of the legislation was that it exempted self-funded employer health insurance policies from state regulations on insurance companies and state premium taxes.

6 Play-or-pay proposals offer employers a choice: Insure your employees or pay into a fund that will cover them.

7 Medi-Cal buy-in refers to allowing low-wage employees who do not meet the criteria for Medi-Cal eligibility to purchase Medi-Cal coverage at subsidized rates.

8 Unless otherwise noted, all citations of MRMIB's position derive from its August 7, 1991 position paper (Major Risk Medical Insurance Board 1991). Positions of the California Association of Health Underwriters are laid out in its statement of November 24, 1991 (California Association of Health Underwriters 1991a).

9 Kaiser had first pitched the concept of pooling small employers at a meeting of the National Association of Insurance Commissioners (NAIC). A 1991 NAIC report on guaranteeing access in the small group market included Kaiser's proposal as one of six approaches (National Association of Insurance Commissioners Health Care Insurance Access Advisory Committee 1991).

10 Multiple-Employer Trusts, also called Multiple Employer Welfare Arrangements, can provide an alternative pathway to coverage for small businesses, but they exist in something of a regulatory vacuum. Many of the trusts are formed by third-party administrators (TPAs) who form them on a "self-funded" basis — premiums are intended to cover the claims, but no actual insurance is purchased to ensure that this occurs. The TPAs claim to be exempt from state regulation under ERISA, making it difficult for state regulators to track them and enforce state laws. The morass of regulatory authority over METs and the financial damage they have wrought is now recognized — between 1988 and 1991, 400,000 participants lost over \$123 million (General Accounting Office 1992) — but the problem is complex and solutions to date have been incomplete.

11 A waiting period is a time during which the enrollee does not pay premiums and does not receive any benefits.

12   For example, the Castro district in San Francisco is primarily homosexual, with a higher-than-average incidence of HIV and associated higher medical care costs.

13   Garamendi was the first elected insurance commissioner for California. Proposition 103 of 1988, the ballot initiative that rolled back automobile insurance premiums, also created an elected insurance commissioner to replace the previously appointed office.

14   PPOs are Preferred Provider Organizations and POS plans refer to Point of Service. Preferred provider organizations are health plan products that offer a discount for visits to members of the "preferred provider" network; enrollees can visit nonmembers, but they pay an additional fee for those visits. Point-of-service plans combine HMOs with preferred provider organizations: For visits inside the HMO network, the enrollee pays only a small copayment; for visits to preferred providers outside the HMO network, the enrollee pays significantly more; and visits to providers outside both networks are most costly.

15   Of course, the end to preferential treatment for associations went both ways — those associations that had been receiving worse-than-average rates on a relatively high-risk membership would have benefited from AB 1672. It is not clear whether any such associations existed; if they did, they would have been satisfied with the effects of AB 1672 and would have had no reason to voice objection.

16   The MRMIB staff runs two other purchasing pools in addition to the HIPC: The Major Risk Medical Insurance Program is the state-run pool for high-risk individuals, and the Access for Infants and Mothers program provides insurance to low-income pregnant women and their newborn babies.

17   Although independent employer groups larger than 50 cannot join the HIPC, such groups that belong to guaranteed associations are allowed to join. Further, independent groups that join the HIPC with fewer then 50 employees and then grow are allowed to stay until the first open-enrollment period at which they exceed 100 enrollees.

18   During the development phase of the HIPC agent compensation scheme, the agent check-off box began as a series of subjective criteria to assess whether the agent had in fact assisted the employer. Under agent protest, the subjective criteria plan became a check-off box indicating that the employer HAD used an agent; further protest resulted in a check-off box indicated that the employer HAD NOT used an agent (Association of California Life Insurance Companies 1993). The subtleties involved in the simple question of whether or not an agent had aided the employer in the enrollment process indicate the stakes involved in these negotiations — or at least the stakes that were perceived in these negotiations.

19   The first-year commissions are as follows: $50 for 3–9; $75 for 10–20; $100 for 21–30; $125 for 31–40; $150 for 41–50; and $175 for 51 or more enrollees. During the second and subsequent years, the agent receives $30 for groups of 3–25, $40 for 26–50, and $50 for 51 or more enrollees (Health Insurance Plan of California 1996–97).

20   Although a detailed analysis is beyond the scope of this paper, Buchmueller (1996a; 1996b) provides extensive information on HIPC enrollment figures and trends in premiums and growth.

21   Recall that the HIPC's compensation scheme makes no provisions for general agents; they are completely cut out of the HIPC's marketing and enrollment system.

22   Marmor et al. define a political market as "institutional arrangements — the relationships among organized pressure groups, voters, authoritative governmental agencies, and affected citizens — that determine what governments do" (Marmor et al. 1981 p. 146).

23   Theoretically, this would win them the speakership. However, Speaker Willie Brown convinced Republican Paul Horcher to convert to an Independent, tying the Assembly at 39 seats each (with one vacancy). Horcher's conversion and support won Brown the speakership until Horcher was recalled. Brown maneuvered to retain his power two more times,

with Republicans Doris Allen and Brian Setencich, until the Republicans finally wrested control from Brown and elected Curt Pringle to the speakership. In the words of one Capitol reporter: "While the long-term impact of Brown's tactical maneuvering will be left for historians to decipher, the short-term effect is indisputable: chaos" (Scott 1995 pp. 12–13).

References

AB 1672 Conference Committee. (1992). "Analysis of the Carrier Coalition Proposal."

Aetna Life and Casualty. (1990). "Access to Health Care: A Proposal for a Public/Private Solution."

Alpha Center. (1996). "Technical Assistance Memorandum #9: Health Insurance Market Reforms and Pooled Purchasing: Select State Provisions."

Association of California Life Insurance Companies. (1991a). Memorandum to ACLIC Uninsured Health Care Task Force, August 30.

Association of California Life Insurance Companies. (1991b). Memorandum to ACLIC Uninsured Task Force, November 25.

Association of California Life Insurance Companies. (1991c). Summary of Health Access Legislation, 1991–1992 Legislative Session, October 11.

Association of California Life Insurance Companies. (1992a). Memorandum to ACLIC Health Care Task Force, April 22.

Association of California Life Insurance Companies. (1992b). Memorandum to ACLIC Health Care Task Force: Health Care Access Issue in California, January 6.

Association of California Life Insurance Companies. (1992c). Memorandum to ACLIC Health Care Task Force: Summary and Status of Pending 1992 California Health Insurance Legislation, April 9.

Association of California Life Insurance Companies. (1992d). Memorandum to ACLIC Uninsured Health Care Task Force, May 11.

Association of California Life Insurance Companies. (1993). "Memorandum to ACLIC Health Care Task Force." January 26.

Association of California Life Insurance Companies. (undated). "Small Group Purchasing Pools in California: A Position Paper by the Association of California Life Insurance Companies."

Block, A.G. (1990). "Budget Deadlock Takes State to the Brink." *California Journal*, September, 420–424.

Blue Cross of California. (1991). "Position Opposing S.B. 1060, Kaiser Permanente 'Pooling' Model." August 1.

BNA's Managed Care Reporter. (1996). "In California Small Business Market, Private Program Competes with HIPC." March 27.

Brown, E.R. (1996). "Trends in Health Insurance Coverage in California, 1989–1993." *Health Affairs*, Spring, 118–130.

Brown, E.R., Valdez, R.B., Morganstern, H., Parivash, N., and Hafner, C. (1988). "Changes in Health Insurance Coverage of Californians, 1979–1986." California Policy Seminar, University of California. Berkeley. August.

Buchmueller, T.C. (1996a). "Government Sponsored Employer Purchasing Cooperatives: The Early Experience of the Health Insurance Plan of California." Manuscript.

Buchmueller, T.C. (1996b). "Managed Competition in the Small Group Health Insurance Market: The Early Experience of California's HIPC." Manuscript.

Buchmueller, T.C., and Jensen, G.A. (1996). "Small Group Reform in a Competitive Managed Care Market: The Case of California, 1993 to 1995." Manuscript.

California Assembly Insurance Committee. (1991). "Analysis of AB 755 for Heaing on May 7, 1991."

California Association of Health Underwriters. (1991a). "Carrier Reform Proposals." November 24.

California Association of Health Underwriters. (1991b). "Explanation of Opposition to State Sponsored Small Employer Pooling Mechanisms." November 24.

California Department of Corporations. (undated). "Small Employer Group Reforms: Monitoring of Standard Employee Risk Rates." Report, Required by Health and Safety Code Section 1357.18.

California Department of Insurance. (1993a). "Bulletin 93–3." April 15.

California Department of Insurance. (1993b). "Notice of Proposed Adoption of Emergency Regulations to Implement, Interpret or Make Specific, Provisions of Chapter 1128, Statutes of 1992 (AB 1672), Relating to Small Employer Health Insurance." Emergency Regulations RH–317. June 11.

California Department of Insurance. (1994). "AB 1838 — Background Information." July 14.

California Senate Committee on Insurance Claims and Corporations. (1992). "Analysis of AB 755 (as amended March 2, 1992) for Hearing on July 1, 1992."

California Senate Office of Research. (1988). "Ensuring Universal Access to Health Care: Recent Lessons From Massachusetts." June.

California Statutes. (1992). "Chapter 1128."

Enthoven, A., and Kronick, R. (1989). "Consumer-Choice Health Plan for the 1990s." *New England Journal of Medicine*, 320, 29–37; 94–101.

Eowan, A. (1993). "How AB 1672 Affects Health Insurance Plans." *California Broker*, Submitted January 5.

Freudenheim, M. (1990a). "California Plans Divide Insurers." *New York Times*. May 8.

Freudenheim, M. (1990b). "Health Insurers, to Reduce Losses, Blacklist Dozens of Occupations." *New York Times*. February 5.

Garamendi, J. (1992). Letter to the AB 1672 Conference Committee Members, April 20.

Garrison, J. (1991). "Locked In." *San Francisco Chronicle, Image*. December 15. p. 29.

General Accounting Office. (1992). "Employee Benefits: States Need Labor's Help Regulating Multiple Employer Welfare Arrangements." HRD–92–40. March.

General Accounting Office. (1994). "Access to Health Insurance: Public and Private Employers' Experience With Purchasing Cooperatives." HEHS–94–142. May.

General Accounting Office. (1995). "Health Insurance Regulation: Variation in Recent State Small Employer Health Insurance Reforms." HEHS–95–161FS.

Governor Wilson. (1992). "Governor Wilson's Proposal for Health Care Reform." April 13.

Gunnison, R. B. (1992). "Sacramento Set For Fight on Health Care, Welfare." *San Francisco Chronicle*. January 6.

Hall, C.P., Jr., and Kuder, J.M. (1990). *Small Business and Health Care: Results of a Survey*. The NFIB Foundation, Washington, D.C.

Harman, L. (1995). "Health Insurance Rates Make Small Banks Ill." *San Diego Business Journal*.

Health Access of California. (1990). "The California Health Access Proposal."

Health Care Financing Administration. (1996). *Health Care Financing Review*, Statistical Supplement.

Health Insurance Association of America. (1995). *1994 Sourcebook on Health Insurance Data*. Health Insurance Association of America, Washington, D. C.

Health Insurance Plan of California. (1995–96). "The HIPC Employer Application."

Health Insurance Plan of California. (1996). "Choicewords." September.

Health Insurance Plan of California. (1996–97). "The HIPC Employer Application."

Himmelstein, D.U., and Woolhandler, S. (1989). "A National Health Program for the United States." *New England Journal of Medicine*, 320(2), 102–108.

Institute for Health Policy Solutions. (1995). "A Comparison of Small-Employer Healthplan Purchasing Alliances." Prepared for the Academy of Healthplan Purchasing Cooperatives' Winter Policy Convocation: Tailoring Health Plan Purchasing and Choice Strategies For Your Market, December 7–8, 1995.

Jacobs, J. (1993). "Sabotaging Health Reform." *Sacramento Bee.* June 13.

Kaiser Permanente. (1991). "Chart on Small Business Carrier Insurance Rating Reforms." August.

Kaiser Permanente. (1991). "Statement of the Kaiser Permanente Medical Care Program on Small Group Market Reform." August.

Kershner, V. (1991). "State Economy in Worse Shape Than Predicted." *San Francisco Chronicle.* October 7.

Kingdon, J.W. (1995). *Agendas, Alternatives, and Public Policies.* HarperCollins College Publishers, New York.

Lehrman, S. (1992). "Health Care 'High Noon': Employers, Workers Spar Over Rising Cost of Care." *San Francisco Chronicle.* January 26.

Lindblom, C.E. (1959). "The Science of 'Muddling Through'." *Public Administration Review,* Spring, 79–88.

Lippert, C., and Wicks, E. (1991). "Critical Distinctions: How Firms That Offer Health Benefits Differ From Those That Do Not." Health Insurance Association of America.

Lipson, D. J., and De Sa, J. (1995). "The Health Insurance Plan of California: First Year Results of a Purchasing Cooperative." Alpha Center. Washington, D.C.

Major Risk Medical Insurance Board. (1991). "Small Group Insurance Underwriting Reform and State Sponsored Purchasing Pool." August 7.

Managed Risk Medical Insurance Board. (1993). "Why Associations Should Not Be Exempted From The Requirements of Chapter 1128 (AB 1672)." March 8.

Managed Risk Medical Insurance Board. (1995). Letter to the Commissioner of the Department of Corporations, August 14.

Marmor, T., Whittman, D., and Heagy, T. (1981). "Politics, Public Policy and Medical Inflation." *Politics and Health Care,* J. McKinlay, ed., MIT Press, Cambridge, Massachusetts, 140–157.

Massachusetts Health Security Act of 1988. (1988). "Fact Sheet #1, Universal Health Insurance Provisions."

National Association of Insurance Commissioners Health Care Insurance Access Advisory Committee. (1991). "Final Report." Presented to the NAIC Health Care Insurance Access Working Group of the NAIC Accident and Health (B) Committee. April 9.

Olszewski, L. (1990). "Willie Brown Supports All-Workers Health Plan." *San Francisco Chronicle.* February 22.

Olszewski, L., and Tuller, D. (1990). "Ronald Katz's Insurance Was Canceled Twice Before He Died." *San Francisco Chronicle.* February 26.

Paulson, L.D., and Zeiger, R. (1992). "Blundering Toward a Budget." *California Journal,* September, 425–430.

Reinhardt, U.E. (1989). "Toward a Fail-Safe Health-Insurance System." *Wall Street Journal.* January 11.

Ross, N.L. (1995). "Health Insurance Purchasing Cooperatives: How Does Your Cooperative Grow?" *Journal of the American Society of CLU and ChFC,* 49(5), 72–81.

Russell, S. (1988). "Blue Cross Ends Coverage for 6,400." *San Francisco Chronicle.* March 12.

Russell, S. (1993a). "New Health Plan for Small Firms: Wilson Promotes State Program That Provides Cost-Saving Pool." *San Francisco Chronicle.* May 19.

Russell, S. (1993b). "State Co-op For Insurance Is Proposed." *San Francisco Chronicle.* January 25.

Salzman, E. (1989). "Stand By For A Big Health Battle." *Sacramento Bee*. March 12.

Scott, S. (1995). "Imbalance of Power." *California Journal*, August, 12–16.

Scott, S. (1996). "What Future Pete?" *California Journal*, June, 8–11.

Silverman, C., Anzick, M., Boyce, S., Campbell, S., McDonnell, K., Reilly, A., and Snider, S. (1995). *EBRI Databook on Employee Benefits.*, Employee Benefit Research Institute, Washington, D.C.

Skocpol, T. (1994). "Is the Time Finally Ripe? Health Insurance Reforms in the 1990s." *The Politics of Health Care Reform: Lessons From The Past, Prospects for the Future*, J.A. Morone and G.S. Belkin, eds., Duke University Press, Durham, North Carolina, 57–76.

Sparer, M.S. (1994). "The Unknown States." *The Politics of Health Care Reform: Lessons From The Past, Prospects for the Future*, J. A. Morone and G. S. Belkin, eds., Duke University Press, Durham, North Carolina, 430–439.

Tierney, J.T. (1987). "Organized Interests in Health Politics and Policy Making." *Medical Care Review*, 44(1), 89–118.

Tuller, D. (1989). "Health Coverage Ax to Hit Californians." *San Francisco Chronicle*. February 7. p. C1.

Tuller, D., and Olszewski, L. (1990). "New Crisis in Health Insurance: Higher Premiums, Blacklists Reported." *San Francisco Chronicle*. February 26.

Turem, J.S. (undated). "Small Group Risk Rates Results: The First Year of AB 1672." The California Department of Insurance: A Report to the Assembly Insurance Committee and the Senate Insurance Committee required by Section 10718.6 of the Insurance Code.

Turner, D. (1995). "Small Banks and Their Employees Suffer Skyrocketing Health Insurance Costs Due to State Reform Measure." *Los Angeles Business Journal*.

Wilson, J.Q. (1973). "Organizations and Public Policy." *Political Organizations*, Basic Books, Inc., New York.

Wilson, J.Q. (1980). "The Politics of Regulation." *The Politics of Regulation*, J.Q. Wilson, ed., Basic Books, New York, 357–394.

Winterbottom, C., Liska, D.W., and Obermaier, K.M. (1995). *State-Level Databook on Health Care Access and Financing*. The Urban Institute, Washington, D.C.

3 Effect of Premium on Health Plan Choice in a Purchasing Alliance

Introduction

Although numerous studies of firm-based health plan choice have been performed, a gap remains in studies of small firms. Small firms that provide coverage for employees generally contract with a single insurer for coverage (Morrisey et al. 1994), leaving little opportunity to analyze choice behaviors. This study, analyzing a new source of data from a purchasing cooperative setting featuring broad choice for small firms, begins to fill the gap in this area.

The objective of this study is to explore the relationship between premium, employer contribution, and employee choice among the four health plan categories offered through the purchasing cooperative, the Health Insurance Plan of California (HIPC): Preferred Provider Organization with a standard benefit package, Preferred Provider Organization with a preferred benefit package, Health Maintenance Organization with a standard benefit package, and Health Maintenance Organization with a preferred benefit package. Employees are assumed to first choose between the two types of managed care plans based on their trade-off between the freedom of provider choice that a PPO offers and the low out-of-pocket costs that an HMO provides. Employees then decide between the standard and the preferred benefit packages, given their choice of managed care plan type. Compared to the standard package, the preferred package offers higher monthly premiums and lower cost-sharing: a lower deductible in the case of the PPO, and lower per-visit cost-sharing in the case of the HMO.

Literature Review

The literature includes a number of studies assessing the importance of premium to plan joining and plan switching behaviors. Almost all of these studies have focused on large employers. McGuire (1981) studied a university, and Buchmueller and Feldstein (1996) looked at an entire university system. Welch (1986) used a national database of medium and large firms; Short and Taylor (1989) also used a national database, drawing a sample of employees offered more than one health insurance option from their employers. Feldman and colleagues (1989) looked at a number of large firms in a single city, as did Dowd and Feldman (1994). Barringer and Mitchell (1994) investigated a sample of four plants from a single large firm. One departure from the focus on large firms was Marquis and Long's study of the individual market for health insurance (1995). Yet little research has been done on health plan choice in small firms.

The studies most relevant to this investigation are those that focused on individuals choosing among health plan options and used some measure of premium as an explanatory variable. Because these studies tend to use some form of logistic regression, a brief overview of the concepts and terminology is worthwhile.[1]

Binary logistic regression has a dependent variable that is bounded by zero and one. The independent variables represent characteristics of the "choosers," the individuals making a decision between the options on the dependent variable. If the independent variables instead consist of characteristics of the "choices," the options on the dependent variable, then this model is called a conditional logit or McFadden's logit model. For example, in a choice between a Health Maintenance Organization and a fee-for-service health plan, a binary logit model would feature independent variables that measured the characteristics of the individuals choosing between the plans, such as gender, education, income, and ethnicity. If the model used premium and cost-sharing variables instead of individual characteristics, it would be a conditional logit; these variables vary with the value on the dependent variable rather than with the value on the independent variable. A model that includes both choice and chooser characteristics is called a mixed model. Although these models are conceptually identical, in the sense that independent variables are used to explain patterns of choice among options on the dependent variable, they are modeled and interpreted differently.[2]

When the dependent variable has more than two values, the model is called a multinomial logit. The same distinction between chooser and choice characteristics holds for multinomial models as holds for binary models. That is, a model with only chooser characteristics is called a multinomial logit model; a model with only choice characteristics is called a conditional multinomial logit model, or a discrete choice model; and a model with both types of variables is called a mixed multinomial model. Multinomial models include an assumption termed the "independence of irrelevant alternatives," which holds that the odds ratio for choosing between any two of the options considered remains constant regardless of whether other options are added to the choice set (Maddala 1983). This is often called the "red bus/blue bus" problem due to a common example used to demonstrate the principle. An individual who is offered three transportation options — a red bus, a blue bus, and a car — is not likely to consider each of them as separate options, but rather is likely to consider either bus as one option and the car as another option. The nested multinomial logit model developed by McFadden addresses this issue by allowing for dependence among the choices on the dependent variable (Maddala 1983).

McGuire (1981) used both logit and linear probability methods to model enrollment as a series of two decisions: first, the decision to purchase coverage, and second, the choice between a fee-for-service plan and a prepaid group practice. Barringer and Mitchell (1994) used a multinomial conditional logit model to assess selection among four options: a Health Maintenance Organization, a traditional fee-for-service plan, a catastrophic fee-for-service plan, and an intermediate fee-for-service plan. Both premium and deductible were included as explanatory variables. Welch (1986), looking at the choice between a Health Maintenance Organization and a fee-for-service Blue Cross plan, used HMO market share as the dependent variable. Out-of-pocket premium and levels of copayments and deductibles were included as independent variables. Short and Taylor (1989) used binary conditional logit models to assess two choices: between two different fee-for-service plans, and between a fee-for-service plan and a Health Maintenance Organization. Feldman and coauthors (1989), performing the most methodologically complex of the studies mentioned here, used a nested multinomial logit model to investigate employee health plan selection from among a large number of options.

As the literature has evolved, a number of issues have arisen. One of them is violations of the independence of irrelevant alternatives (IIA) assumption in estimation of multinomial logit models. Feldman and colleagues assert that when multiple options of each type of plan are offered to an individual, they should not all be assumed to be equivalent alternatives (Feldman et al. 1989). That is, an individual facing a choice of five Health Maintenance Organizations and one fee-for-service plan may not consider them equally; like the red bus/blue bus problem, the HMOs may be seen as one option, compared with the fee-for-service plan. To solve this problem, Feldman and coauthors employ the nested multinomial logit method, grouping the health plan options into two nests: one "freedom of choice" nest (including fee-for-service plans and independent practice association HMOs) and one nest of traditional HMOs. This allows the investigators to test the assumption that individuals differentiate between the two types of health plans. However, use of this model has disadvantages as well. It is significantly more complex and more difficult to interpret than is a conditional multinomial logit model. Thus, the increase in precision comes at the cost of reduced transparency and accessibility. Alternatively, the multinomial logit model employed by Barringer and Mitchell does not differentiate fee-for-service and HMO "nests," but provides interpretable and intuitive results. Another approach has been to reduce the options among which the individual chooses by eliminating choices until the individual is left with only two (Short and Taylor 1989; Welch 1986), but this tactic requires that the analysis disregard valid data. The study described in this chapter avoids the independence of irrelevant alternatives problem by using a sequential logit model, which will be discussed in section 4.

Another problem that arises is whether full data are available on the choice set faced by the individual. An individual who is single and has no dependents will consider only a single-coverage plan. However, married individuals who are each offered coverage through the workplace face a different choice: Both enroll in the plan offered through workplace A, both enroll in the plan offered through workplace B, and both enroll in the single-coverage plan offered through their separate workplaces (given that both will purchase coverage). If they choose the latter option, they will look exactly like the single employee who had no other options to consider. Thus, an analysis that looks at all individuals who chose single-coverage plans may be ignoring options considered but not chosen by those who enrolled.

Although this problem must be acknowledged, it cannot always be addressed. Optimally, the researcher would have complete data on all options considered by all individuals in the dataset. This is somewhat unrealistic, since it includes detailed data from multiple employers. More accessible, but still demanding, is obtaining data on whether alternative options are available, even if full data on the options are not available (*e.g.*, information on whether the married couple has two workplace options but no information on the characteristics of the options). More realistic is information on marital status and dependents that allows the researchers to separate out subsets of individuals facing the same choice. Feldman and colleagues, in the only study among those mentioned to address this problem, had both the second and the third categories of data: information on whether workers had alternative options through spouses, and marital/dependent status (Feldman et al. 1989). They chose two subsets for analysis. Unmarried employees with no dependents were assumed to consider only single coverage. Single-parent families and married workers whose spouses were not covered through employment were assumed to consider only family coverage. Unfortunately, since the HIPC data include neither information on alternative options nor marital status, this problem cannot be addressed. Like many other studies (Barringer and Mitchell 1994; Short and Taylor 1989; Welch 1986), the decision among alternative family categories is taken as given; HIPC enrollees are assumed to choose only among the options in the family category that they actually chose.

Data

The Health Insurance Plan of California was created as part of a package of reforms in the health insurance market for firms with between 3 and 50 employees, California Assembly Bill 1672. AB 1672, passed in 1992 and implemented in July 1993, imposed stringent regulations on the small group market, including guaranteed issue and renewal of all products, rating restrictions, and limitations on pre-existing condition exclusions. The regulations apply to the HIPC as well as to the small group market. The Managed Risk Medical Insurance Board (MRMIB), a state agency, is responsible for the HIPC. The Board and its staff handle policy decisions and negotiations and contracting with participating health plans; daily operations are contracted out to Employers Health Insurance, which handles enrollment, marketing, and data collection.

The health plans participating in the HIPC use a grid of six regions, four family groups, and seven age groups to set premiums. This rating structure, in conjunction with the fact that the HIPC offers only four types of health plans (preferred PPO, standard PPO, preferred HMO, and standard HMO) allows the HIPC to publish its rates in an annual brochure without qualifications about possible adjustments for health status or other factors. Table 3.1 shows a rate grid for Employee-Only plans in Region 1 for the 1994–1995 benefit year. Region 1 has three other grids for the three other family groups: Employee and Spouse, Employee and Child(ren), and Family. The other five regions all have four similar grids, but the number of plans available to enrollees varies among the HIPC's six regions.

The data for this study come from the HIPC's enrollment files, and contain information on employers, employees, and dependents. The unit of analysis for the study is the employee. The dataset includes all employees who joined the HIPC during its second year of operation, between July 1, 1994 and June 30, 1995. The employers of these employees are included in the database, regardless of when the employers first joined the HIPC. That is, if the employer joined the HIPC in August 1993 and added an employee in April 1995, the employee and the employer will both be included in the dataset. The dependents of the employees are also included if they joined the HIPC within 30 days of the employee. The reason for the time limit is plan selection: The employee's initial choice of health plan is influenced by the type (spouse or child) and number of dependents. Dependents who joined the HIPC long after the employee joined would not have been taken into account in the employee's initial choice of plan. The cutoff date was set at one month based on the assumption that 30 days was a reasonable delay to attribute to processing paperwork. Enrollees 65 or more years of age are excluded from the analysis for two reasons. First, they are likely to be quite different from the vast majority of the over-65 population because they are obtaining their primary health care coverage through the HIPC rather than through Medicare. Second, there are very few enrollees in this age category: just 151 out of over 40,000 enrollees, comprising less than one-half of one percent of the 1994–95 enrollment.

Because the enrollment data collection was designed for administration rather than research, several problems result. One problem is that for some variables, new variable values overwrite the old values. For example, each employer is asked about the firm's number of employees. When the question is repeated on the application the following year, the old values are overwritten in the databank. For this analysis, firm size was estimated by

TABLE 3.1   1994–1995 Monthly Premiums for Region 1 Employee-Only Plan

	Age Group						
	<30	30–39	40–49	50–54	55–59	60–64	65+
Standard HMO							
Cigna Private	84.30	92.57	110.02	144.38	182.71	236.59	278.16
Health Net	104.74	120.35	145.58	186.88	239.56	295.84	287.28
Kaiser North	89.29	89.29	113.15	150.13	181.35	215.06	250.68
National HMO	85.50	104.50	122.55	154.85	187.15	229.00	255.00
Omni	94.21	110.75	134.79	166.41	210.84	258.46	251.66
Pacificare	115.03	113.15	127.39	190.27	230.49	288.92	234.32
Prucare	101.00	126.00	145.00	184.00	221.00	253.00	316.00
Takecare	117.87	134.83	151.52	179.51	213.55	233.46	249.18
Standard PPO							
Aetna	104.61	104.61	132.00	174.54	210.41	249.08	290.03
EHI	74.00	90.00	112.00	148.00	181.00	198.00	153.00
John Alden	93.04	102.05	131.43	173.33	218.92	265.56	288.16
Preferred HMO							
Cigna Private	91.94	100.96	120.00	157.48	199.28	258.03	303.36
Health Net	113.65	130.59	157.97	202.78	259.94	321.02	311.73
Kaiser North	101.05	101.05	124.91	161.89	193.11	226.82	262.44
National HMO	101.65	115.90	136.80	171.00	203.30	255.00	290.00
Omni	103.72	121.95	148.41	183.23	232.16	282.65	277.09
Pacificare	121.15	119.97	135.44	202.84	245.71	307.99	252.85
Prucare	108.00	134.00	154.00	195.00	235.00	269.00	336.00
Takecare	128.51	149.86	165.20	195.72	232.83	254.66	271.68
Preferred PPO							
Aetna	111.73	111.73	140.97	186.40	224.72	266.02	309.75
EHI	80.00	98.00	122.00	162.00	198.00	217.00	167.00
John Alden	107.27	117.65	151.52	199.82	252.39	306.16	332.22

Source: Health Insurance Plan of California, Employee Brochure and Application (1994–1995).

counting the number of employees with the same employer identification number who joined the HIPC during the 1994–1995 year. This figure will underestimate the true figure because not all of each firm's employees join the HIPC; some employees have alternative sources of coverage or simply decline coverage. However, the counting method should provide a close approximation.

Second, the variable measuring the employer's contribution to the employee's premium is imprecise. To join the HIPC, employers must contribute at least 50 percent of the premium of the lowest-cost employee-only plan. But employers are free to contribute more than that: They may contribute 50 percent toward the purchase of the lowest-cost plan in each family group, *i.e.*, subsidize dependent coverage, or they may contribute 50 percent toward any plan at all, including the most costly plan. The application does not ask the employer to specify the firm's contribution policy; it simply asks what percentage contribution the firm makes. Without specifying to which premium the percentage contribution applies, there is no way to link the contribution to a specific category of plan. To further complicate matters, some employers contribute a fixed sum rather than a percentage; to answer the question on the application, they may calculate the percentage contribution using some denominator of their own choosing, or they may write in the fixed contribution, in which case the HIPC personnel convert it into a percentage value. In short, the employer contribution variable is very muddy. A third problem is that some variables that are important for this study but not for database administration are missing, most important, income data.

An issue that is worth briefly noting relates to trade and professional associations. The HIPC enrolls firms with 3–50 employees, and allows such firms to stay enrolled until they exceed 100 employees. However, state law also permits firms that belong to certain trade and professional associations to join the HIPC, regardless of the size of the firm. Thus, some of the enrollees in the HIPC work for firms with more than 100 employees, and some are self-employed. Unfortunately, the HIPC considered association membership to be sensitive information, precluding the identification and differentiation of firms that joined the HIPC through an association. However, given that the employee is the unit of analysis rather than the employer, and that the study looks at the employee choice of plan rather than at the employer choice of whether to join the HIPC, association membership should not be overly problematic.

In spite of these problems, the data present a rare opportunity to investigate employee-level choice in the small group market. Descriptive statistics are presented in Tables 3.2–3.4. Table 3.2 compares the data by region; Table 3.3 looks at family group; Table 3.4 compares those who joined HMOs to those who joined PPOs, and those who had prior insurance to those who did not. Table 3.5 lists the counties that are included in each of the HIPC's six regions across the state. Region 1 is rural, region 2 is somewhat less rural, and regions 3–6 are urban.

Model

The complete process of enrollment in the HIPC is assumed to unfold in four stages:

Stage 1: The employer decides to join the HIPC
Stage 2: The employee decides between an HMO and a PPO
Stage 3: The employee decides between a standard and a preferred benefit package
Stage 4: The employee selects a plan from among the options in the chosen category

Unfortunately, although the employer's decision to join the HIPC, purchase insurance in the outside market, or forego insurance coverage for employees is an interesting and important topic for study, no data are available on Stage 1.

The focus of this analysis is Stages 2 and 3. These stages address the key question: the impact of premiums and employer contribution on choice of plan type. The rationale for this framework is that because HMOs and PPOs differ, they cannot be considered as like alternatives. Preferred Provider Organizations offer much more extensive provider choice, both because they tend to have very broad networks and because the plans provide some degree of coverage for out-of-network providers. For the privilege of choice, PPO enrollees share more of the costs of care with the plan than do HMO enrollees. By contrast, HMOs are characterized by a restricted provider panel, no out-of-network coverage, and lower levels of cost-sharing. Cost-sharing requirements for the two types of plans are displayed in Table 3.6. Cost-sharing in PPOs begins with a deductible, which is paid entirely by the enrollee. After meeting the deductible, the enrollee pays coinsurance, or

TABLE 3.2   Descriptive Statistics for HIPC Population, 1994–1995, N=40,037, By Region

	All Regions (n=40,037)	Region 1 (n=1,082)	Region 2 (n=4,625)	Region 3 (n=15,192)
Age, Mean (years)	36.7	38.0	36.8	36.3
Age Group (%)				
< 30	32	26	31	33
30–39	33	32	33	33
40–49	22	28	24	22
50–54	6	7	6	6
55–59	4	5	4	3
60–64	2	2	2	2
Family Group (%)				
Employee Only	68	55	60	70
Employee and Spouse	10	12	11	9
Employee and Child	8	9	10	7
Family	15	23	19	14
Number of Children, Mean	.44	.65	.58	.39
Number of Children, Range	0–11	0–5	0–8	0–7
Nonwhite (%)	42	28	36	45
Female (%)	46	41	45	45
Previously Uninsured (%)	24	26	24	21
Employer's Contribution to Premium (% Mean)	82	85	83	85
Employers Contributing Greater than Minimum (%)	76	82	75	81
Employers Using an Agent (%)	73	66	74	77
Number of PPOs Offered	3	3	3	3
Number of HMOs Offered	19	8	12	12
Type of Coverage (%)				
PPO, preferred	8	11	7	6
PPO, standard	3	6	2	2
HMO, preferred	53	53	58	56
HMO, standard	36	30	34	36
Monthly Premium, Mean ($)	185	225	195	180

a percentage of the price of each medical service consumed. In an HMO, copayments take the place of both deductible and coinsurance; copayments are small fixed sums paid at the time of utilization of medical services. The

TABLE 3.2 Descriptive Statistics for HIPC Population, 1994–1995, N=40,037, By Region (continued)

	All Regions (n=40,037)	Region 4 (n=4,015)	Region 5 (n=7,093)	Region 6 (n=8,030)
Age, Mean (years)	36.7	36.5	36.1	37.7
Age Group (%)				
< 30	32	33	35	29
30–39	33	32	32	31
40–49	22	21	20	25
50–54	6	6	6	7
55–59	4	4	4	5
60–64	2	3	3	3
Family Group (%)				
Employee Only	68	66	73	65
Employee and Spouse	10	11	8	11
Employee and Child	8	8	8	8
Family	15	15	12	16
Number of Children, Mean	.44	.44	.37	.47
Number of Children, Range	0–11	0–5	0–11	0–8
Nonwhite (%)	42	35	54	34
Female (%)	· 46	44	48	48
Previously Uninsured (%)	24	26	30	23
Employer's Contribution to Premium (% Mean)	82	80	80	81
Employers Contributing Greater than Minimum (%)	76	72	71	72
Employers Using an Agent (%)	73	69	67	74
Number of PPOs Offered	3	3	3	3
Number of HMOs Offered	19	14	14	13
Type of Coverage (%)				
PPO, preferred	8	11	9	11
PPO, standard	3	5	4	2
HMO, preferred	53	45	51	51
HMO, standard	36	39	36	36
Monthly Premium, Mean ($)	185	190	180	186

coinsurance of PPOs is a more open-ended type of cost-sharing than is the copayment contribution used by HMOs; for a hospital visit, 20 percent of the bill (40 percent for out-of-network coverage) is likely to amount to a

TABLE 3.3 Descriptive Statistics for HIPC Population, 1994–1995, N=40,037, By Family Group

	Employee Only (n=27,054)	Family (n=6,005) (n=3,816)	Employee and Spouse	Employee and Child(ren) (n=3,162)
Age, Mean (years)	35.5	38.5	43.0	36.0
Age Group (%)				
< 30	39	14	18	26
30–39	30	45	24	41
40–49	19	34	25	28
50–54	6	6	14	3
55–59	4	1	11	1
60–64	2	0	8	0
Number of Children, Mean	0	2.0	0	1.6
Number of Children, Range	0	1–11	0	1–7
Nonwhite (%)	42	41	34	47
Female (%)	50	24	37	61
Previously Uninsured (%)	28	13	16	22
Employer's Contribution to Premium (% Mean)	82	84	84	81
Employers Contributing Greater than Minimum (%)	75	80	79	75
Employers Using an Agent (%)	73	74	76	71
Type of Coverage (%)				
PPO, preferred	8	10	11	5
PPO, standard	2	3	5	2
HMO, preferred	54	51	47	58
HMO, standard	36	35	37	35
Premium, Mean ($)	117	391	299	240

much more significant contribution than the $100 required for a hospitalization in an HMO with a standard benefit package. The trade-off can be summarized as follows: provider choice, with higher out-of-pocket costs and greater financial exposure in the PPO, or restricted choice with lower out-of-pocket costs and less financial risk in the HMO. Conceptualization of this stage of the analysis follows the precedent set in the literature for this distinction (Barringer and Mitchell 1994; Feldman et al. 1989; McGuire 1981).

TABLE 3.4 Descriptive Statistics for HIPC Population, 1994–1995, N=40,037, By Plan Choice and Prior Insurance Status

	HMO Members (n=35,607)	PPO Members (n=4,367)	Previously Insured (n=30,406)	Previously Uninsured (n=9,631)
Age, Mean (years)	36.1	41.2	37.6	33.6
Age Group (%)				
< 30	34	17	28	45
30–39	33	31	33	30
40–49	22	29	24	17
50–54	6	11	7	4
55–59	4	6	4	3
60–64	2	5	3	1
Family Group (%)				
Employee Only	68	63	64	78
Employee and Spouse	9	14	11	6
Employee and Child	8	5	8	7
Family	15	18	17	8
Number of Children, Mean	.43	.44	.48	.29
Number of Children, Range	0–11	0–6	0–11	0–9
Nonwhite (%)	43	30	38	53
Female (%)	46	47	48	38
Previously Uninsured (%)	26	8	0	100
Employer's Contribution to Premium (% Mean)	82	87	84	78
Employers Contributing Greater than Minimum of 50 Percent (%)	75	82	78	67
Employers Using an Agent (%)	73	71	73	74
Type of Coverage (%)				
PPO, preferred	0	76	10	3
PPO, standard	0	24	3	0
HMO, preferred	60	0	54	52
HMO, standard	40	0	33	45
Premium, Mean ($)	178	243	197	149

Once the individual has made the trade-off between more extensive provider choice in PPOs and more comprehensive coverage of out-of-pocket costs in HMOs, the next step is to decide between the standard and preferred

TABLE 3.5   Location of California Counties in HIPC's Six Regions

Region 1 (n=1,082)	Alpine	Monterey
	Amador	Nevada
	Butte	Placer
	Calaveras	Plumas
	Colusa	San Benito
	Del Norte	Shasta
	El Dorado	Sierra
	Glenn	Siskiyou
	Humboldt	Sutter
	Inyo	Tehama
	Kings	Trinity
	Lake	Tulare
	Lassen	Tuolumne
	Mendocino	Yolo
	Modoc	Yuba
	Mono	
Region 2 (n=4,625)	Fresno	Sacramento
	Imperial	San Joaquin
	Kern	San Luis Obispo
	Madera	Santa Cruz
	Mariposa	Solano
	Merced	Sonoma
	Napa	Stanislaus
Region 3 (n=15,192)	Alameda	San Francisco
	Contra Costa	San Mateo
	Marin	Santa Clara
Region 4 (n=4,015)	Orange	Ventura
	Santa Barbara	
Region 5 (n=7,093)	Los Angeles	
Region 6 (n=8,030)	Riverside	San Diego
	San Bernardino	

Source: Health Plan of California, Employee Brochure and Application (1994–1995).

benefit packages. Table 3.6 summarizes the differences in the HIPC benefit packages for PPOs and HMOs. It is important to note that the benefit package is the same for the standard and preferred options; the only difference between the two packages is in the level of cost-sharing. The preferred HMO offers a lower copayment for office visits and inpatient admissions than does the standard package (*e.g.*, $5 for a preferred package office visit and $15 for a standard package office visit). The preferred PPO offers a lower deductible ($250 per person for the preferred package and $500 per person for the standard package). To balance out the lower levels of cost-sharing offered in the preferred packages, those packages feature higher monthly premiums than do the standard packages. Thus, each employee must make a trade-off between paying a higher sum up-front in monthly premiums or paying more throughout the year as services are needed. Note that this decision is somewhat different for HMO-choosers than it is for PPO-choosers. For PPOs, the difference between the standard and preferred packages is limited to the deductible amount; once the deductible is reached, cost-sharing for services is exactly the same for both plan options. This is not so for HMOs, which have no deductible but ongoing differences in the amount paid for services.

The breadth and depth of the delivery network provided by the plan and the quality of services provided are unobserved variables in this analysis. However, it seems likely that these factors play the most important role after the general category of health plan has been selected, at the point when the individual selects a specific plan from those offered in the chosen category. For example, having chosen a preferred HMO, the individual then selects a specific preferred HMO from those offered, and quality and network considerations would come into play more prominently here than they would in selection of a broad category of plan. Selection of a specific plan, Stage 4 in our model, is beyond the scope of the current analysis. Stage 4 requires a conditional multinomial logit analysis for each plan category — standard HMO, preferred HMO, standard PPO, preferred PPO. This would allow estimation of price elasticities among plans of the same category.

Obviously, some HIPC enrollees do not choose their health plan in accordance with the decision stages presented here. For example, a satisfied Kaiser Permanente member whose employer joins the HIPC may not consider any other health plan. However, it seems plausible that many HIPC enrollees first choose a broad category of health plan, based on the value they place on freedom of choice of provider, and then make a trade-off

TABLE 3.6   Cost-Sharing For HIPC Benefit Packages

	HMO*	PPO*
Yearly Deductible	$0	$500/$250 per person
Yearly Out-of-Pocket Maximum	$2000 per person $4000 per family	*in network:* $2000 per person $4000 per family *out of network:* $5000 per person $10,000 per family
Physician Services	$15/$5 per visit	20% in network 40% out of network
Hospital Services	$100/$0 per admission	20% in network 40% out of network
Prescription Drugs	$10/$5 per generic rx $15/$10 per brand rx	20% per generic rx 30% per brand name rx
Emergency Services	$50 if not admitted to hospital	20%, plus $50 if not admitted to hospital
Prenatal and Infant Visits	$5 per visit	0% in network 40% out of network
Outpatient Services for Occupational, Physical, & Speech Therapists	$15/$5 per visit	20% in network 40% out of network
Home Health Services	$15/$5 per visit	20% in network 40% out of network
Preventive Health Services	$15/$5 per visit	20% in network 40% out of network
Durable Medical Equipment	$0	20% in network 40% out of network
Mental Health Services	$100/$0 per admission $20 per visit	20% per inpatient admission in network; 40% per inpatient admission out of network; 50% in or out of network for outpatient services
Chemical Dependency Services	$100/$0 per admission Outpatient costs vary	20% per inpatient admission in network; 40% per inpatient admission out of network; all costs over $20 per visit for outpatient services
Infertility Services	40% of contracted or scheduled rate	50% in or out of network

* If Standard and Preferred benefits differ, they are given as Standard/Preferred. Only the deductible differs for the PPO plans.

Source: Health Insurance Plan of California, Employee Brochure and Application (1994–1995).

between higher up-front costs with lower cost-sharing at time of treatment and lower premiums with larger payments for the deductible or visit charges.

Although it may not precisely mirror reality, the hypothesized decision structure is more intuitively appealing than an alternative selection process that has been presented in the literature: "We assume that the decision-making process begins with the employee asking him- or herself the following hypothetical (*i.e.*, conditional) questions: 'If I were to sign up for a plan at work and if I elect family coverage, which HMO would be best for me? Which traditional plan would be best?'" (Short and Taylor 1989, p. 296). The authors assert that the individual will choose hypothetically between the best HMO and the best fee-for-service plan offering family coverage, and then will repeat the process for single coverage. Having chosen the best family coverage plan and the best single-coverage plan, the individual decides between those two. The final decision is between the chosen plan, a spouse's coverage, or no insurance. This structure is an example of backward induction, which is, in game theory terminology, a "dynamic game of complete and perfect information" (Gibbons 1992, p. 57). Although the assumption of complete and perfect information may work well for simple games, such information is not available in the selection of health plans, nor is the strong assumption of rationality that underlies this process justified.

Methodology

Having addressed the logic of the model, we turn to the methodology. Modeling the choice between a PPO and an HMO followed by the choice between a standard or preferred benefit package can be performed using a sequential logit model. As long as the decisions at later stages are independent of the decisions at earlier stages, a series of binary logit models is appropriate. In this case, we will first model the choice of HMO or PPO, using the entire dataset. Next, we run two more binary logits: one for those who chose a PPO in the first stage, and one for those who chose an HMO in the first stage. The outcome variable in each of the two latter models is choice between a standard and a preferred benefit package.

We assume choice of plan type and choice of benefit package are independent. The choice between PPO and HMO involves a trade-off: those who choose provider choice must also be willing to pay higher cost-sharing amounts and to accept greater exposure to financial risk.[3] By contrast, the choice between standard and preferred benefit packages presents a different trade-off, between higher monthly premiums with lower payments at time of utilization and lower premiums but a larger deductible or visit charges. A counterargument to independence of the two stages is the assertion that health status drives both stages. Although it is likely that health status drives the choice between standard and preferred packages, it is unlikely that this is a strong factor in the choice between HMO and PPO. When choosing between standard and preferred packages, those who expect to be high utilizers of medical services are likely to choose the preferred package because they will likely save more in avoided cost-sharing than they will pay in additional premiums. This is particularly true for those who enroll in HMOs, since the difference in cost-sharing for HMOs is open-ended, while the difference in cost-sharing for PPOs is restricted to the deductible. However, those who expect to be high utilizers of medical services may choose either HMOs or PPOs. High utilizers who have established relationships with providers may prefer to stay with those providers, and so would choose a PPO. Alternatively, high utilizers may prefer the greater financial security of HMO coverage — maintaining established provider relationships through a PPO can be costly, particularly if the providers are outside the PPO network.

The Binary Logit Model

Each of the two decisions — HMO or PPO, standard or preferred benefit package — can be conceptualized as a relationship between an unobserved variable, y^*, and a series of x characteristics associated with each employee (Judge et al. 1988; Liao 1994; Maddala 1983):

$$y^* = \sum_{k=1}^{K} \beta_k x_k + \varepsilon$$

The outcome variable, y, will take on the value:

1   if $y^* > 0$
0   otherwise.

The unobserved y^* can be seen as a threshold level of utility: if, for example, the utility of joining a PPO outweighs that of joining an HMO, the threshold is crossed and the employee joins a PPO. Otherwise, the employee joins an

HMO. The threshold itself cannot be observed, and may be different for each employee.

Assuming that the error term, ε, has the logistic distribution, the result is a logit model. The binary logit model takes the form

$$\ln \frac{P(y=1)}{1-P(y=1)} = \sum_{k=1}^{K} \beta_k x_k$$

with the log of the odds ratio (also called the logit) on the left-hand side of the equation. In this case, the regression coefficients represent the change in the log of the odds ratio (the odds, for example, of choosing a PPO versus choosing an HMO). Since predicted probabilities are more intuitively appealing than is the log of the odds, the equation can be transformed as follows:

$$P(y=1) = \frac{e^{\sum_{k=1}^{K} \beta_k x_k}}{1+e^{\sum_{k=1}^{K} \beta_k x_k}}$$

This equation yields the predicted probability of an outcome of 1 on the dependent variable (choosing a PPO), given the values of the independent variables.

Final Probabilities in the Sequential Logit Model

Once the binary logit regressions have been run, the chain rule for probabilities can be used to calculate the final probabilities associated with each of the four types of health plans: preferred PPO, standard PPO, preferred HMO, and standard HMO. The chain rule for probabilities states that the probability for events A and B both occurring is equivalent to the probability of event A occurring times the probability of event B occurring, given that A has already occurred:

Pr(A,B) = Pr(A) × Pr(B|A)

Thus, the probability that an employee chooses a preferred PPO is equal to the product of the probability of choosing a PPO and the probability of choosing a preferred benefit package, given the prior choice of a PPO. Final probabilities for each of the other three types of plans can be calculated similarly, substituting $1 - \mathrm{Pr(A)}$ for $\mathrm{Pr(A)}$ when the employee chooses an

HMO and $1 - Pr(B)$ for $Pr(B)$ when the employee chooses a standard benefit package.

Variables

Descriptive statistics for the variables used in the three regressions are presented in Tables 3.7–3.9. The dependent variable for the first equation is PPO; a value of 1 represents enrollment by the employee in a Preferred Provider Organization, while a value of 0 represents enrollment in a Health Maintenance Organization. The dependent variable for the second and third regressions is PREFER; a value of 1 represents enrollment by the employee in a preferred benefit package, while a value of 0 represents enrollment in a standard benefit package. Each equation includes two cost variables and a number of employee characteristics.

The cost variables are a measure of relative premium for the different plan types and a measure of the employer's contribution to the employee's premium. The relative premium is calculated by comparing the two types of plans that are assumed to be under consideration in each of the three equations. For the first equation, the outcome variable indicates whether the employee joined a PPO or an HMO. The relative premium variable in that equation is determined by first calculating the average premium of each of the two plan types for each region, family, and age combination. Since there are 6 regions, 4 family groups, and 6 age categories,[4] there are a total of $6 \times 4 \times 6 = 144$ average premiums for HMOs, and 144 average premiums for PPOs. For example, the average premium for an HMO in region 3 for a 34-year-old employee with a spouse in the HIPC is $243.34, while the average PPO premium is $253.89. For a 55-year-old employee with a family in region 1, the average HMO premium is $568.89 while the average PPO premium is $511.98. The relative premium variable for the first equation is calculated by dividing each of the 144 PPO premiums by its counterpart HMO premium. The variable is then multiplied by 100. The result expresses the average premium of a PPO in a given region/age/family category as a percent of the average premium of an HMO in that category. For the two examples above, the variable values are 108.341 and 89.996. That is, for the 34-year-old, the average PPO premium is 108 percent of the average HMO premium. For the 55-year-old, the average PPO premium is 90 percent of the average HMO premium. This variable is denoted PCTP_H.

TABLE 3.7   Descriptive Statistics for Regression Variables, Logit on Choice Between HMO and PPO, N=40,037

Variable	Definition	Mean	Std Deviation
Independent			
PCTP_H	Ratio of average premium of PPO to average premium of HMO, in each region/age/family combination, expressed as a percent	109.83	13.05
MEDCTRB	Employer's contribution to employee's premium, expressed as a percent	82.41	20.64
NONWHITE	1 if Nonwhite / 0 if White	.42	.49
FEMALE	1 if Female / 0 if Male	.46	.50
PRIORINS	1 if previously insured 0 if previously uninsured	.76	.43
AGE	Age, in years	36.7	10.6
AGE SQ	Age squared	1457.48	844.02
SPOUSE	1 if spouse enrolled in HIPC 0 otherwise	.25	.43
NUMCHILD	Number of dependent children enrolled in the HIPC	.44	.92
TOTALEE	Number of employees in company that joined HIPC in 1994–95	17.54	20.02
REGION1	1 if employee resides in region 1 0 otherwise	.027	.162
REGION2	1 if employee resides in region 2 0 otherwise	.116	.320
REGION3	1 if employee resides in region 3 0 otherwise	.379	.485
REGION4	1 if employee resides in region 4 0 otherwise	.100	.300
REGION5	1 if employee resides in region 5 0 otherwise	.177	.382
REGION6	1 if employee resides in region 6 0 otherwise	.201	.400
Dependent			
PPO	1 if employee joined a PPO 0 if employee joined an HMO	.109	.312

TABLE 3.8   Descriptive Statistics for Regression Variables, Logit on Choice Between Standard and Preferred Benefit Packages Among PPO Choosers, N=4,367

Variable	Definition	Mean	Std Deviation
Independent			
PCTPP_SP	Ratio of average premium of preferred PPO to standard PPO, in each region/age/family combination, expressed as a percent	109.85	.41
MEDCTRB	Employer's contribution to employee's premium, expressed as a percent	86.53	19.15
NONWHITE	1 if Nonwhite / 0 if White	.31	.46
FEMALE	1 if Female / 0 if Male	.47	.50
PRIORINS	1 if previously insured 0 if previously uninsured	.92	.27
AGE	Age, in years	41.2	10.7
AGE SQ	Age squared	1813.94	912.35
SPOUSE	1 if spouse enrolled in HIPC 0 otherwise	.32	.47
NUMCHILD	Number of dependent children enrolled in the HIPC	.44	.91
TOTALEE	Number of employees in company that joined HIPC in 1994–95	14.02	16.15
REGION1	1 if employee resides in region 1 0 otherwise	.041	.199
REGION2	1 if employee resides in region 2 0 otherwise	.087	.281
REGION3	1 if employee resides in region 3 0 otherwise	.274	.446
REGION4	1 if employee resides in region 4 0 otherwise	.145	.352
REGION5	1 if employee resides in region 5 0 otherwise	.214	.410
REGION6	1 if employee resides in region 6 0 otherwise	.239	.426
Dependent			
PREFER	1 if a preferred package chosen 0 if a standard package chosen	.760	.427

TABLE 3.9   Descriptive Statistics for Regression Variables, Logit on Choice Between Standard and Preferred Benefit Packages Among HMO Choosers, N=35,670

Variable	Definition	Mean	Std Deviation
Independent			
PCTPH_SH	Ratio of average premium of preferred HMO to standard HMO, in each region/age/family combination, expressed as a percent	111.56	1.16
MEDCTRB	Employer's contribution to employee's premium, expressed as a percent	81.90	20.75
NONWHITE	1 if Nonwhite / 0 if White	.43	.49
FEMALE	1 if Female / 0 if Male	.46	.50
PRIORINS	1 if previously insured 0 if previously uninsured	.74	.44
AGE	Age, in years	36.1	10.4
AGE SQ	Age squared	1413.84	824.77
SPOUSE	1 if spouse enrolled in HIPC 0 otherwise	.24	.42
NUMCHILD	Number of dependent children enrolled in the HIPC	.44	.92
TOTALEE	Number of employees in company that joined HIPC in 1994–95	17.97	20.40
REGION1	1 if employee resides in region 1 0 otherwise	.025	.157
REGION2	1 if employee resides in region 2 0 otherwise	.119	.324
REGION3	1 if employee resides in region 3 0 otherwise	.392	.488
REGION4	1 if employee resides in region 4 0 otherwise	.095	.292
REGION5	1 if employee resides in region 5 0 otherwise	.173	.378
REGION6	1 if employee resides in region 6 0 otherwise	.196	.397
Dependent			
PREFER	1 if a preferred package chosen 0 if a standard package chosen	.597	.490

A similar process was followed for the relative premium variables for equations in the next stage — the choice between a standard and a preferred benefit package for the HMO choosers, and the same choice for the PPO choosers. For each of the 144 cells, four values were calculated: the average premium of a preferred PPO, the average premium of a preferred HMO, the average premium of a standard PPO, and the average premium of a standard HMO. The relative premium variable for the PPO-choosers' regression was the ratio of the average premium of a preferred PPO to the average premium of a standard PPO, again multiplied by 100 to create a percentage variable. The relative premium variable for the HMO-choosers' regression was the average premium of a preferred HMO divided by the average premium for a standard HMO, times 100. Continuing with our example from above, assume that the 34-year-old has chosen an HMO and the 55-year-old has chosen a PPO during the first stage. During the second stage, the ratio for the 34-year-old's region/age/family group is 113.067, indicating that the average premium for a preferred HMO is 113 percent more than for a standard HMO. For the 55-year-old, a value of 110.569 signifies that the average preferred PPO costs 110.6 percent more than the average standard PPO. The relative premium variable comparing the preferred to the standard PPO is denoted PCTPP_SP; the comparable HMO variable is PCTPH_SH.

The employer contribution variable is more straightforward but may be less useful; recall that this variable is quite imprecise. It is simply the percent contribution to the employee premium that has been reported by the employer on the HIPC's Employer Application. The employers are required to contribute at least 50 percent of the employee-only premium for the lowest-cost plan in the employee's region and age group but may contribute

TABLE 3.10   Distribution of the Employer Contribution Variable

MEDCTRB Employer Contribution to Premium	Frequency Number (Percent) of Employees, N=40,037
50%	9,690 (24.2%)
51–99%	14,397 (36%)
100%	15,950 (39.8%)

more. The distribution of employer contribution variable, MEDCTRB, is presented in Table 3.10. The majority of employees work for firms that contribute either 50 or 100 percent; the mean contribution is 82.4 percent. The variable that the employer reports may refer strictly to a percent of the employee-only premium for the lowest-cost plan, or it may refer to the lowest-cost plan in any family category that the employee chooses. It may also refer to any plan at all that the employee chooses. Thus, interpretation of any results associated with this variable are subject to caution.

Employee characteristics included in the regressions are the following: ethnicity, gender, whether the employee had health insurance prior to joining the HIPC, age, whether the employee has a spouse who is enrolled in the HIPC, and how many (if any) of the employee's children are enrolled in the HIPC. Firm size is estimated by the number of fellow employees who also joined the HIPC during the 1994–95 benefit year. Geographical differences are captured by five dummy variables. These variables are identical for the three regressions.

The variables of primary concern for interpretation are the relative premium variables (PCTP_H, PCTPP_SP, and PCTPH_SH) and the employer contribution variable (MEDCTRB). In each equation we expect a negative coefficient for the premium index variable, signifying that the probability of enrolling in a type of plan decreases as its relative premium increases. Expectations for the employer contribution are less clear-cut, because they depend on whether the contribution applies to the lowest-cost plan or to the plan of the employee's choice, which is unknown. Most often, the lowest-cost plan is an HMO; this is the case for all six age groups in regions 3–6, for all but one age groups in region 2, and for half of the age groups in region 1. If the contribution applied to the lowest-cost plan, the employee would be required to pay the full marginal cost of upgrading to the higher-premium PPO. By contrast, if the contribution applied to the plan of the employee's choice, the employer would partially subsidize the employee's choice of a PPO. Thus, a strong association between employer contribution and choice of PPO might indicate that the employer was contributing toward the employee's choice of plan rather than toward the lowest-cost option. But the employer pays no part of the higher out-of-pocket costs associated with a PPO, which means that an employee who is relatively indifferent to freedom of provider choice will prefer to apply the flexible employer contribution to a higher-cost HMO than to a PPO.

In the choice between a standard and a preferred benefit package, the uncertainty regarding the employer's contribution policy likewise prevents definitive anticipation of results. If the contribution applies to any benefit package, the employee would pay only a fraction of the marginal cost of the increased premium of a preferred package, which would yield lower out-of-pocket costs for the employee. But if the employer tied contributions to the low-cost package, the entire cost of upgrading from a standard to a preferred package would be borne by the employee. Thus, a strong association between employer contribution and choice of preferred package might indicate that the contribution applied to the package of the employee's choice.

Results

Logit for Choosing Between PPO and HMO

The results of the first regression are presented in Table 3.11. The sample size for this regression is 40,037 employees, 11 percent of whom chose a PPO. The coefficients in a logit regression do not give the change in predicted probability of a value of 1 on the outcome variable associated with a one-unit increase in the independent variable; rather, they give the change in the log of the odds ratio of a value of 1 compared to a value of 0 on the outcome variable that is associated with a one-unit increase in the independent variable. Thus, only the direction of the impact on the outcome variable can be ascertained from the logit coefficient, not the magnitude of the effect. Magnitude is approximated by the far-right column of the table, labeled "Marginal Probability." This value gives the effect of a one-unit increase in the independent variable on the predicted probability of a value of 1 on the dependent variable. The magnitude of the effect of the independent variables changes with the value of the variables; marginal probability gives the effect on the predicted probability at a specific value of the independent variable. For continuous variables, marginal probabilities are calculated by evaluating the predicted probability of a value of 1 on the dependent variable at the sample mean of all the independent variables, and then increasing the value of the independent variable of concern by 1 unit and recalculating the predicted probability (Petersen 1985). The difference between the two predicted probability values represents the impact of increasing the independent variable by 1 from the sample mean, holding all

TABLE 3.11   Logit Results for Choice Between HMO and PPO, Dependent Variable = PPO (0=HMO, 1=PPO)

Variable	Parameter Estimate	Standard Error	Significance Level	Marginal Effect on Probability* (in percent)
INTERCEPT	−2.6001	0.4709	0.0001	
PCTP_H	−0.0339	0.00429	0.0001	−0.257
MEDCTRB	0.00779	0.000869	0.0001	0.0599
NONWHITE	−0.3117	0.0363	0.0001	−2.348
FEMALE	0.03	0.0344	0.3822	
PRIORINS	1.2546	0.0592	0.0001	7.5909
AGE	0.095	0.0116	0.0001	.7584
AGE SQ	−0.00067	0.000138	0.0001	
SPOUSE	0.2357	0.0433	0.0001	1.9013
NUMCHILD	−0.2275	0.0263	0.0001	−1.588
TOTALEE	−0.00822	0.00108	0.0001	−0.063
REGION2	−0.6288	0.1018	0.0001	−3.97
REGION3	−0.4007	0.1026	0.0001	−2.964
REGION4	0.985	0.1532	0.0001	10.5041
REGION5	1.253	0.1903	0.0001	13.5808
REGION6	0.1564	0.1067	0.1427	

Sample Size = 40,037
Chi-Square for covariates = 2363.9 (p=.0001)

* Marginal Probability is calculated only for statistically significant variables (p<=.05). It is not calculated for age squared because the interpretation of marginal probability is not intuitive for this variable.

other variables constant at their sample means. The same procedure is followed for discrete variables, except that the predicted probabilities are calculated at values of 0 and 1 on the discrete independent variables rather than at the sample mean and at the sample mean plus 1.

As expected, the coefficient for the relative premium variable is negative and significant. The value for marginal probability indicates that as the average PPO premium increases by 1 percent relative to the average HMO premium, the probability of joining a PPO decreases by .257 percent. Since the marginal probability gives only the incremental effect of the relative premium variable at the sample mean, the table below provides additional information. Table 3.12 and Chart 3.1 show that as the average premium of a PPO increases relative to the average premium of an HMO, the impact on the probability of joining a PPO lessens. When the average premium of a PPO increases from 80 percent to 90 percent of the average premium of an HMO, the probability of joining a PPO drops by 4.9 percent, from 20 to 15.1

TABLE 3.12   Effect of Relative Premium on Predicted Probability of Joining a PPO

PCTP_H	Probability (PPO)	Change in Prob (PPO)
80	0.200644	
90	0.151707	−0.048937
100	0.113018	−0.038689
110	0.083228	−0.02979
120	0.060752	−0.022476
130	0.044054	−0.016698
140	0.031791	−0.012263
150	0.022859	−0.008932

CHART 3.1   Effect of Relative Premium on Predicted Probability of Joining a PPO

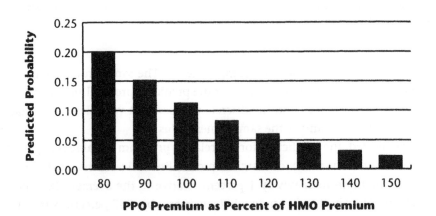

percent. However, when the average premium of a PPO increases from 140 to 150 percent of the average premium of an HMO, the probability of joining a PPO drops by just 0.9 percent, from 3.2 to 2.3 percent.

The employer's contribution to the premium has a positive and significant effect on the probability of joining a PPO, indicating that employees are more likely to join PPOs as the premium contribution from their employers increases. The magnitude of the effect, however, is very small, with a marginal probability of just .000599. This signifies that an increase in employer contribution from 82.4 percent of premium to 83.4 percent of

TABLE 3.13   Effect of Employer Contribution on Predicted Probability of Joining a PPO

MEDCTRB	Probability (PPO)	Change in Prob (PPO)
50	0.066305	
60	0.071293	0.004988
70	0.076626	0.005333
80	0.082323	0.005697
90	0.088403	0.00608
100	0.094885	0.006482

CHART 3.2   Effect of Employer Contribution on Predicted Probability of Joining a PPO

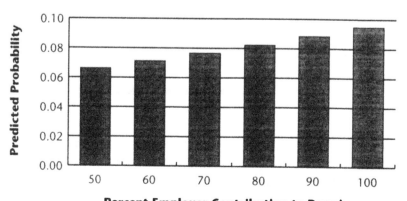

premium is associated with a .06 percent increase in the probability of joining a PPO. Table 3.13 and Chart 3.2 show that enrollment in PPOs increases very slightly but steadily with increasing employer contribution.

All of the other variables in the model are also highly significant, with the exception of gender and the dummy variable for region 6. Enrollees of nonwhite ethnicity are 2.3 percent less likely to join a PPO than are white enrollees. Having a spouse enrolled in the HIPC increases the probability of joining a PPO by 1.9 percent, but an additional child decreases the probability by 1.6 percent. A variable with a particularly strong impact is PRIORINS, indicating whether the employee had health insurance prior to joining the HIPC. Employees with prior insurance are 7.6 percent more likely to join PPOs than are those without. Chart 3.3 plots predicted probability of joining a PPO against relative premium, by prior insurance status. The PRIORINS variable may be picking up the effect of income, an unobserved variable in the analysis.

CHART 3.3   Effect of Relative Premium on Predicted Probability of Joining a PPO, By Prior Insurance Status

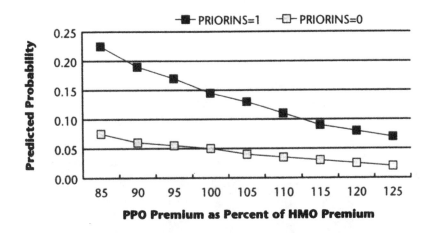

Age and age squared are both highly significant; together they demonstrate that the probability of joining a PPO increases with age but at a decreasing rate. The relative premiums of PPO and HMO also impact employees of various ages to different degrees, as Chart 3.4 below shows.

CHART 3.4 Effect of Relative Premium on Predicted Probability of Joining a PPO, By Age

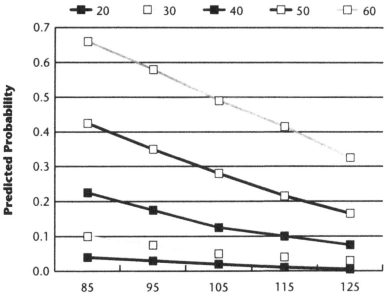

PPO Premium as Percent of HMO Premium

Logit for Choosing a Benefit Package

Having decided to enroll in an HMO or a PPO, employees must then decide between a standard and a preferred benefit package. Two regressions were run, one for PPO choosers and one for HMO choosers, both with the variable PREFER as the outcome variable (1 if the employee chose a preferred package, and 0 if a standard one). The PPO-choosers regression had a sample size of 4,367, 76 percent of whom chose a preferred package; Table 3.14 shows the results. The HMO-choosers regression had a sample size of 35,670, 59 percent of whom chose a preferred package; Table 3.15 shows the results.

Again, the key variables for interpretation are relative premium and employer contribution. In neither of these regressions, however, does the relative premium variable approach statistical significance. Most likely, there is insufficient variation in the 144 region/family/age cells for the relative premium variables that compare the preferred and standard premiums. The variable comparing the premiums of preferred and standard PPOs,

TABLE 3.14   Logit Results for Choice Between Standard and Preferred Benefit Packages Among PPO Choosers, Dependent Variable = PREFER (0=STANDARD, 1=PREFER)

Variable	Parameter Estimate	Standard Error	Significance Level	Marginal Effect on Probability* (in percent)
INTERCEPT	−13.226	36.4248	0.7165	
PCTPP_SP	0.1049	0.3319	0.752	
MEDCTRB	0.00476	0.00188	0.0115	0.082757
NONWHITE	0.0455	0.081	0.5744	
FEMALE	0.1575	0.0777	0.0427	2.733227
PRIORINS	0.1797	0.1331	0.177	
AGE	0.0965	0.026	0.0002	1.634357
AGE SQ	−0.00145	0.000294	0.0001	
SPOUSE	−0.1757	0.0971	0.0704	−3.11017
NUMCHILD	0.0477	0.0526	0.3642	
TOTALEE	0.023	0.00311	0.0001	0.397657
REGION2	0.7792	0.209	0.0002	11.20092
REGION3	0.7901	0.1986	0.0001	12.4093
REGION4	0.3575	0.3285	0.2765	
REGION5	0.369	0.3745	0.3245	
REGION6	0.9636	0.1974	0.0001	14.49461

Sample Size = 4,367
Chi-Square for covariates = 262.5 (p=.0001)

* Marginal Probability is calculated only for statistically significant variables (p<=.05). It is not calculated for age squared because the interpretation of marginal probability is not intuitive for this variable.

PCTPP_SP, ranges from 109.0 to 110.8, with a mean of 109.95 and a standard deviation of only 0.45. The variable comparing the premiums of preferred and standard HMOs, PCTPH_SH, has slightly more variation, ranging from 103.4 to 113.1 with a mean of 110.4 and a standard deviation of 1.43. It appears that, on average, the plans price their preferred options at 10 percent more than their standard options, with little variation. The variation in neither variable approaches that of the statistically significant PCTP_H, the

TABLE 3.15   Logit Results for Choice Between Standard and Preferred Benefit Packages Among HMO Choosers, Dependent Variable = PREFER (0=STANDARD, 1=PREFER)

Variable	Parameter Estimate	Standard Error	Significance Level	Marginal Effect on Probability* (in percent)
INTERCEPT	2.5499	2.8224	0.3663	
PCTPH_SH	−0.0276	0.0262	0.2936	
MEDCTRB	0.00852	0.000534	0.0001	0.202549
NONWHITE	−0.0916	0.0228	0.0001	−2.18229
FEMALE	0.2848	0.0226	0.0001	6.74967
PRIORINS	0.2985	0.0256	0.0001	7.19433
AGE	0.00951	0.00769	0.216	
AGE SQ	−0.00027	0.000097	0.0052	
SPOUSE	−0.1095	0.031	0.0004	−2.62072
NUMCHILD	0.0318	0.0149	0.0324	0.753949
TOTALEE	0.00386	0.000553	0.0001	0.091849
REGION2	0.0106	0.0986	0.9147	
REGION3	−0.0536	0.1257	0.6697	
REGION4	−0.341	0.0851	0.0001	−8.30666
REGION5	−0.1332	0.0897	0.1374	
REGION6	−0.1274	0.1009	0.2064	

Sample Size = 35,670
Chi-Square for covariates = 880.6 (p=.0001)

* Marginal Probability is calculated only for statistically significant variables (p<=.05). It is not calculated for age squared because the interpretation of marginal probability is not intuitive for this variable.

variable that compares the relative premiums of PPOs and HMOs: that variable ranges from 83.3 to 148.9 with a mean of 109.1 and a standard deviation of 15.56.

The employer contribution variable is significant in both regressions, but again its magnitude is quite small. Both HMO-choosers and PPO-choosers are more likely to choose a preferred benefit package over a standard package as the employer contribution to premium increases, but employer contribution — at least this imprecisely measured version — does not appear to be a driving factor. The weakness of the effect may signify that the employers are contributing to the low-cost plan rather than to the plan of the employee's choice. If the contribution could be used for any plan, the employee would have an incentive to upgrade from standard to preferred because preferred plans have higher premiums — which would be partially offset by the employer contribution — and lower cost-sharing, which the employee must pay out of pocket. However, if the employer contribution were restricted to the low-cost plan, the additional premium cost of upgrading from standard to preferred would be paid entirely by the employee.

Both HMO-choosers and PPO-choosers are more likely to select a preferred benefit package if they are women (about 7 percent and 3 percent more likely, respectively), and are less likely to select a preferred package if they have a spouse enrolled in the HIPC (about 3 percent less likely for both). Those in relatively large firms are more likely to choose preferred packages than are those in smaller firms, but the magnitude of this effect is small. Among those who chose HMOs, but not among those who chose PPOs, the probability of selecting a preferred benefit package is higher among those who are white and had prior insurance; each child enrolled in the HIPC increases it slightly. Among those who chose PPOs, but not among those who chose HMOs, the probability of selecting a preferred rather than a standard benefit package increases with age. Neither regression shows a particular pattern of plan type selection among the geographical regions.

Final Probabilities in the Sequential Logit

Calculating the final probabilities associated with joining the four types of plans can be done using the chain rule for probabilities, $\Pr(A,B) = \Pr(A) \times \Pr(B|A)$. We define events A and B as:

Event A = choose PPO
Event not A = choose HMO
Event B = choose preferred package
Event not B = choose standard package

Then, the combination of those events yields the four probabilities of interest:

Probability (Preferred PPO) = Event (A,B) = Pr(A)*Pr(B|A)
Probability (Standard PPO) = Event (A, not B) =Pr(A)*Pr(*notB*|A)
Probability (Preferred HMO) = Event (not A, B) =Pr(*notA*)*Pr(B|*notA*)
Probability (Standard HMO) = Event (not A, not B) =Pr(*notA*)*Pr(*notB*|*notA*)

Evaluated at the sample means for all independent variables, Table 3.16 below shows the predicted probabilities for joining the four types of plans. It also shows the actual proportions of the sample that joined each plan type. While not exact, the predicted probabilities are quite close to the actual proportions.

TABLE 3.16   Final Probabilities in the Sequential Logit (calculated at sample means for all independent variables)

	Predicted Probability (Calculated from Logit Results)	Actual Proportion
Preferred PPO	.064992	.082898
Standard PPO	.018755	.026176
Preferred HMO	.558749	.532008
Standard HMO	.357504	.358918

The key objective of this study was to investigate the impact of relative premium on selection behavior at each stage in the decision-making process, and the cumulative effect across stages. Although the findings for the first stage are interesting, the lack of variation in the relative premiums of preferred and standard benefit packages results in statistically nonsignificant parameters, precluding any findings regarding the effect of relative premium in the second stage. The lack of variation in relative premiums also prevents assessment of the influence of relative premiums on the final probabilities, because it is not valid to calculate the premium effect on the final probabilities when the second-stage probabilities are statistically nonsignificant. However, the impact of employer contribution to premium on the final probabilities of enrolling in the four plan types are presented below. Table 3.17 displays predicted probabilities and Chart 3.5 graphically represents the trend: As employer contribution increases, employees substitute away from standard HMOs and toward preferred HMOs and PPOs.

TABLE 3.17   Effect of Employer Contribution on Predicted Probability of Joining Plan Types

Employer Contribution (%)	Prob (Preferred PPO)	Prob (Preferred HMO)	Prob (Standard PPO)	Prob (Standard HMO)
50	0.049331	0.507539	0.016973	0.426157
60	0.054	0.524	0.018	0.404
70	0.058	0.54	0.018	0.383
80	0.063	0.556	0.019	0.362
90	0.069	0.571	0.02	0.341
100	0.075	0.585	0.02	0.321

CHART 3.5   Effect of Employer Contribution on Predicted Probability of Joining Plan Types

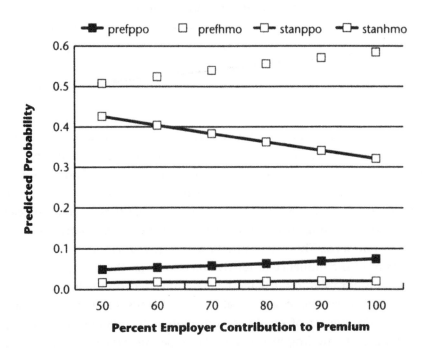

Another finding worth brief note is the impact of age on the probability of joining the various plan types. Age comes into play most strongly in later decades; while probabilities remain relatively unchanged during the 20s and 30s, they change fairly dramatically during the 40s and 50s, with preferred PPOs gaining relative to preferred HMOs and standard HMOs. This relationship is shown below, in Chart 3.6.

CHART 3.6   Effect of Age on Predicted Probability of Joining Plan Types

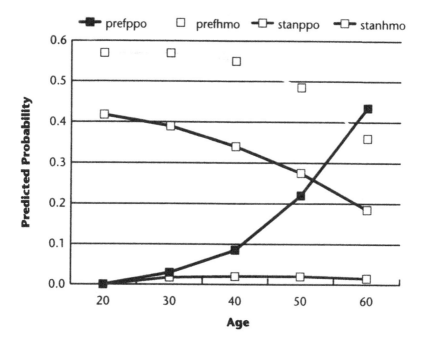

A final finding is the association between prior insurance and choice of health plan. As Chart 3.7 shows, those with prior insurance are more likely than those without to join preferred HMOs, preferred PPOs, and standard PPOs; those without prior insurance are far more likely to join standard HMOs. Again, this may reflect an unobserved income effect.

Discussion and Conclusion

This analysis shows that premium has an important effect on the choice of type of health plan among small firm employees in a purchasing cooperative

CHART 3.7 Predicted Probability of Joining Plan Types, By Prior Insurance Status

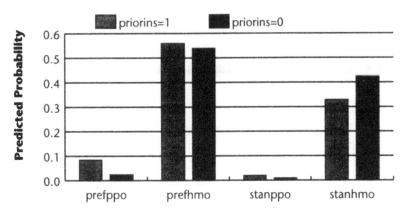

Percent Employer Contribution to Premium

setting that provides a broad selection of plans. Employees were more likely to enroll in HMO plans as HMO premiums dropped relative to PPO premiums. Employer contribution was also found to be a contributing factor in the choice of plan type, although of relatively small magnitude. As employer contribution increased, the probability of joining a PPO instead of an HMO increased slightly. Likewise, the probability of selecting a preferred rather than a standard benefit package increased with employer contribution, regardless of whether HMO or PPO had been chosen in the first stage.

The results of the first stage of the analysis — the choice between HMO and PPO — provide some confirmatory evidence that the trade-off may be perceived as one between the provider choice available in a PPO and the lower and less risky cost-sharing available in an HMO. Holding premium constant, the probability of joining an HMO is higher for those who are younger, of nonwhite ethnicity, and who had no health insurance when they joined the HIPC. All three variables are likely correlated with income, which was missing from the analysis: Those who are older, white, and had prior health insurance are likely to have a higher income level. One interpretation might be that the young, nonwhite, and previously uninsured join HMOs because they have lower premiums than do PPOs, which is often the case. However, it is worth emphasizing that PPO premiums are not necessarily higher than HMO premiums — in many cases, they are lower. It is the cost-sharing feature of PPOs that makes them more costly, and more financially risky, than are HMOs. Thus, an alternative interpretation of the results is that the young, nonwhite, and previously uninsured join HMOs because they provide lower cost-sharing and less exposure to large out-of-pocket payments than do PPOs. The variable measuring the number of dependent children fits in with this interpretation as well — the coefficient for this variable indicated that employees with more children enrolled in the HIPC are more likely to join HMOs. The PPO deductible can add up quickly, costing an additional $250 or $500 per child (depending on whether the standard or preferred benefit package was chosen) before the health plan begins to contribute to medical care costs; even after the deductible, paying 20–40 percent of the cost of pediatrician visits may translate into significant financial outlays.

The second stage of the analysis — the choice between standard and preferred benefit packages — was somewhat less interesting. When averaged within region/age/family group combinations, preferred packages were approximately 10 percent more costly than were standard packages, with little variation. Lack of variation in relative premium for preferred and standard benefit packages resulted in an inability to detect the effect of premium on choice of benefit package, precluding interpretation of the effects of relative premium on the final probabilities of selection among the four categories of health plan (preferred PPO, standard PPO, preferred HMO, and standard HMO).

This study helps to address the paucity of information available regarding choice of health plan among small firm employees. Researchers interested in investigating choice in a small firm context face a common obstacle in that the majority of small firms that provide health care coverage offer only one option to their employees. This study accesses a rare source of data on choice among a wide selection of options for small firms.

Notes

1   Researchers sometimes differentiate between logistic regression and logit, using the term logistic to refer to regressions on continuous independent variables and logit to refer to regressions on discrete (dummy) independent variables. Since this differentiation can be more confusing than useful, the terms will be used interchangeably here.

2   The key difference in interpretation is that a conditional logit model with choice attributes as the independent variables results in coefficients for the independent variables that are

constant across response categories. Thus, the analysis results in a single parameter for each independent variable regardless of the number of categories on the dependent variable. This is not the case in a logit model with chooser characteristics as the independent variables. Coefficients for chooser characteristics do vary across response categories, and analysis produces a separate set of coefficients for each response category.

3   Exposure to financial risk is not extreme in either case, because both HMOs and PPOs limit the out-of-pocket costs that can be incurred by enrollees. However, for PPO members who go out of network, the out-of-pocket maximums can be quite high. Refer to Table 6 for further detail.

4   There are actually seven age categories, but recall that the >65 age category has been eliminated from the study.

References

Barringer, M.W., and Mitchell, O.S. (1994). "Workers' Preferences Among Company-Provided Health Insurance Plans." *Industrial and Labor Relations Review*, 48(1), 141–152.

Buchmueller, T.C., and Feldstein, P.J. (1996). "Consumers' Sensitivity To Health Plan Premiums: Evidence From a Natural Experiment in California." *Health Affairs*, 15(1), 143–151.

Dowd, B., and Feldman, R. (1994). "Premium Elasticities of Health Plan Choice." *Inquiry*, 31, 438–444.

Feldman, R., Finch, M., Dowd, B., and Cassou, S. (1989). "The Demand for Employment-Based Health Insurance Plans." *Journal of Human Resources*, 24, 115–142.

Gibbons, R. (1992). *Game Theory for Applied Economists*. Princeton University Press, Princeton.

Health Insurance Plan of California. (1994–1995). "The HIPC Employee Brochure and Application."

Judge, G.G., Hill, R.C., Griffiths, W.E., Lutkepohl, H., and Lee, T.C. (1988). *Introduction to the Theory and Practice of Econometrics*. John Wiley and Sons, New York.

Liao, T.F. (1994). *Interpreting Probability Models: Logit, Probit, and Other Generalized Linear Models*. Sage Publications, Thousand Oaks.

Maddala, G.S. (1983). *Limited-Dependent and Qualitative Variables in Econometrics*. Cambridge University Press, Cambridge.

Marquis, M.S., and Long, S.H. (1995). "Worker Demand for Health Insurance in the Non-Group Market." *Journal of Health Economics*, 14, 47–63.

McGuire, T.G. (1981). "Price and Membership in a Prepaid Group Medical Practice." *Medical Care*, 19(2), 172–183.

Morrisey, M.A., Jensen, G.A., and Morlock, R.A. (1994). "Small Employers and the Health Insurance Market." *Health Affairs*, 13(5), 149–161.

Petersen, T. (1985). "A Comment on Presenting Results From Logit and Probit Models." *American Sociological Review*, 50(1), 130–131.

Short, P.F., and Taylor, A.K. (1989). "Premiums, Benefits, and Employee Choice of Health Insurance Options." *Journal of Health Economics*, 8, 293–311.

Welch, W.P. (1986). "The Elasticity of Demand for Health Maintenance Organizations." *Journal of Human Resources*, 21(2), 252–266.

Index

For Product Safety Concerns and Information please contact our EU
representative GPSR@taylorandfrancis.com Taylor & Francis Verlag GmbH,
Kaufingerstraße 24, 80331 München, Germany

Printed and bound by CPI Group (UK) Ltd, Croydon, CR0 4YY
08/05/2025
01864399-0001